AMERICA FIRST

Americans Must Come Together For Freedom

Roy Bain

iQ InfoQuest

Available in Digital

ISBN 979-8-9912031-0-4 (Paperback)
ISBN 979-8-3304-8098-2 (Hardcover)

Copyright © 2024 by Roy Bain

All Rights Reserved. No part of this publication may be reproduced, distributed, or transmitted in any form or by any means, including photocopying, recording, or other electronic or mechanical methods without the prior written permission of the publisher. For permission requests, solicit the publisher via the address below.

Publify Publishing

Lampasas, TX 76550

contact@publifypublishing.com

The Library of Congress has cataloged this edition as follows:

Bain, Roy "America First, Americans Must Come Together For Freedom"/ Roy Bain

DEDICATION

This book is dedicated to Democrats, Republicans, Libertarians, and Independents. We may not all share the same approach as to how we must save our democracy, but we are all patriotic **AMERICANS** and now is the time we must all come together to save the **FREEDOM** we all love.

To my wonderful wife of over sixty years

 Jean

Have I told you you're the most important person in my life?
Have I told you I'm so lucky to have you as my wife?
Have I told you all the many, many things you are to me?
Well, just in case I haven't told you lately, let me mention two or three.
You are the sunshine in my morning; you are the smile upon my face.
You are the lover in my evening, in your gowns of silk and lace.
You are the sweet scent of the flower that I stop to smell.
It's your strength that gives me power that I shall never fail.
Did I tell you when I found you, you were the object of my cares?
Did I tell you when I found you, you were the answer to my prayers?
Did I tell you that I loved you, oh so long ago?
Well, just in case I haven't told you lately, it's time I let you know.
I love you because you're kind to every living thing.
I love your positive mind and all the happiness you bring.
I love you, you're my best friend, and that you'll always be.
And, most of all, I love you for the way that you love me.

CONTENTS

CHAPTER ONE - What this book is all about 1

CHAPTER TWO - Calvin Coolidge 16

CHAPTER THREE - Herbert Hoover 36

CHAPTER FOUR - Franklin Delano Roosevelt 48

CHAPTER FIVE - And then there was me 74

CHAPTER SIX - Harry S Truman 83

CHAPTER SEVEN - Dwight D. Eisenhower 103

CHAPTER EIGHT - John Fitzgerald Kennedy 122

CHAPTER NINE - Lyndon Baines Johnson 149

CHAPTER TEN - Richard Milhous Nixon 163

CHAPTER ELEVEN - Gerald R. Ford 182

CHAPTER TWELVE - Looking Back Fifty Years 187

CHAPTER THIRTEEN - James Earl "Jimmy" Carter 191

CHAPTER FOURTEEN - Ronald W. Reagan 208

CHAPTER FIFTEEN - George H.W. Bush 234

CHAPTER SIXTEEN - William Jefferson Clinton 242

CHAPTER SEVENTEEN - George Walker Bush 259

CHAPTER EIGHTEEN - Barack Hussein Obama II 272

CHAPTER NINETEEN - Donald J. Trump 295

CHAPTER TWENTY - Joseph Robinette Biden Jr. 321

CHAPTER TWENTY ONE - Choices, Choices, Choices 342

CHAPTER TWENTY TWO - Conclusion 352

CHAPTER ONE

What this book is all about

The characters and events in this book are non-fictitious. They are past and present living people, and the events are factual to the best of the author's ability to portray.

At 6:11 p.m. on JULY 13, 2024, there was an assassination attempt on former president and leading 2024 presidential candidate Donald J. Trump. In the past 100 years there have been at least 17 attempts to assassinate the president or candidate for president of the United States. Two attempts were successful. Each attempt is covered in this book including the attempt on Donald J. Trump!

> **"The difference between genius and stupidity is that genius has its limits."**
>
> **...Anonymous**

Allow me to tell you something about the author of this work. At this point, you know absolutely nothing about him. You don't know how he thinks, what he believes or why it is important for you to get to know him.

It takes time to watch a movie and even more time to read a book. You, like the author of this book, have spent your precious time watching a movie or reading a book and come away feeling you just wasted a few hours!

I'm going to tell you about the author, his background and how he believes and why he has authored this book. If after learning a little about the author you do not believe you can gain anything of value from his thoughts, don't waste your precious time. I certainly hope that doesn't happen. However, your time is valuable, and it is the desire of the author to present a cache of valuable and timely historical facts in an interesting manor which will aid you to evaluate the past and prepare your thinking for your future which will have an influence on the future of this nation.

Contrary to common thought, *we are not all created equal!* (Sorry Abraham). *We* are, in fact, all created unequal! When we came down the chute and entered this world, our hardware (our computer) was intact. Some of us were lucky and received excellent hardware, most received mediocre hardware, and some who are unfortunate, got inferior hardware. We didn't select our ancestors, so the hardware we received was all a matter of genetic chance. There is a little of all of them in each of us. At birth our computers were close to empty, our ears are working in the seventh month of pregnancy, and we begin to hear and collect information. After birth we each collected our software differently. Most of us, baring congenital defects, received five senses, touch, taste, smell, vision, and hearing. The purpose of our five senses is to gather information to be sent to our brain, sorted out and stored as knowledge. We feed our body through our mouth, and we feed our brains through our senses. Everything that makes you a knowledgeable person today was sent to your computer via your senses.

With the aging process, as the senses grow dim, the input wanes and the mind grows dim. Many of us are inductive learners, we adapted to our environment receiving the teachings of others through formal education. Others who are deductive learners, gained their knowledge by trial and error. Some received both.

Human intelligence and intellectual potential are often measured by IQ (Intelligence Quotient). Most people in the United States fall between 85 and 115; a small few are above 115 and a small few are below 85. The average American IQ is 100. The exact IQ of the **genius** scientist, Albert Einstein was never determined; however, experts estimate it between 160 to 190.

Now in the author's own words:

While I was attending high school, they conducted IQ tests. My IQ score was 142. They told me I was a **genius**.

Big deal! Being a genius didn't mean much to me at the time considering I was failing almost every class except math and physical exercise. Both math and PE made sense to me. Two plus two is four and it's fun to run and jump. Most of the other subjects, at the time, did not make sense to me. I did not do well in English. I've written twelve books and still don't know how to conjugate a verb. I did poorly in spelling, and thought, "If <u>b-u-r-d</u> doesn't spell bird, what does it spell?" And I never could see a use for algebra, and I still can't. The reason I mention my IQ here is not to impress you. It is to let you know you are spending your time reading a book written by a GENIUS who is a little smarter than the average American.

To be fair I must quote physicist, Stephen Hawking, whose IQ was 160. When he was asked what his IQ was, Hawking said, "I don't know. People who boast about their IQ are losers!" You be the judge.

I was born in 1938 in South San Francisco. The city's Black population rose considerably before and during World War II and I grew up in a predominately Black neighborhood. My birth name is LeRoy. Seems that every other kid I knew was named LeRoy. Jim Crow laws were a part of life and segregation existed big time back then, so while both black and white kids often went to the same schools, we were separated into different classes. We did, however share the same recesses.

Many of my childhood friends were black, many were Italian, and many more were Japanese. While I found most kids friendly, occasionally I had fights with a few of them. I did a lot of running as a kid. When you are running from another kid who wants to beat you up, you don't care what color he is. I learned at an early age to like or dislike others by how they acted, not for what race or color they were. Growing up poor helped me see people in a more equal way. We all had laughing shoes and usually a few holes in our clothes. Laughing shoes were shoes where the soles were partially detached so when you walked the sole would flop together and then apart making a popping, laughing noise.

Roy Rogers and Trigger

As a kid my weekends were often spent at the Granada Theater. King of the Cowboys **Roy Rogers** became my childhood hero, which proved good for me. At a young age I went by my shortened name, Roy, so when I played cowboys with friends, I always got to play the part of the good guy, Roy Rogers. I acted the part and always tried to become the part of the good guy. Roy was my hero all through life, and later, my childhood hero became my best friend for the last twenty years of his life.

Here is one of two poems that I wrote that was hanging in the Roy Rogers and Dale Evans Museum in Victorville, California and then later in Branson, Missouri.

My Hero Forever

Oh, the things that I did when I was a kid,
Still bring back sweet memories to mind.
Daydreaming in Mineral City, I rode the Double R Ranch,
Where good guys always won and bad guys had no chance.
I'd saddle up my faithful ol' broom, ride through moms livin' room.
With a slap on my side, I'd go on my make-believe ride.
The doggies were grazin', my cap guns were blazin'.
Wishin' I was much bigger, and my broom was Trigger.
Every day after school, till daylight was through.
Then mom tucked me in bed singing, "Happy Trails to You."

Back when we were boys, we had no toys.
Pretending to be my hero, was my game.
My friends were Hoppy and Gene, Dale was my Cowgirl Queen.
I played Roy Rogers in my backyard wild western scene.
Proudly in my saddle I sat, wearing my white cowboy hat.
My dog became Bullet, my brother a sidekick named Pat.
Though the years have slipped away, and my hair has turned gray.
What I learned from my Hero, is still with me today.
He taught me to do right in life's every endeavor.
The King of the Cowboys shall be My Hero Forever.

At seven or eight years old, the Bain family left San Francisco and moved to Gonzales, California, a small farming community a hundred or so miles south of San Francisco. At roughly 4:30 a.m. each morning, a two-and-a-half-ton converted army truck stopped a block from our house. My mother, two brothers, two sisters and I, along with a group of farm workers, boarded the truck and left for work in the fields. Because we kids slept in our clothes, we crawled out of bed, washed our face, combed our hair, then stumbled down the street, crawled onto the bench in the back of the truck, and went back to sleep. I will never forget the milk can that was welded to the bed of the truck from which we all drank water all day using the same long-handled dipper. Other times we drank water from the irrigation ditch. When we arrived at a farm, we all sat around a campfire until daylight. Depending on what vegetables were in season, the day was spent topping garlic, bunching carrots, or thinning sugar beets. Topping garlic paid nineteen cents a box. Pictured is my garlic topping sheers, newly painted.

As soon as I filled ten boxes with garlic, which took me until noon, my mom would let me go home. I usually took my younger brother, Don, with me; he was six years old. On our way home, we'd walk through the fields to the highway and then thumb a ride back to town. The farmers picked most vegetables a little green for shipping. A few ripe vegetables were always left in the fields after harvest, so by the time Don and I reached the highway, we were often toting a crate of broccoli, lettuce, or onions we'd gathered along the way. After crawling in the dirt topping garlic, we probably didn't look or smell like anyone you would want in your car, so our ride was usually in the back of a pickup. Once we arrived home, we would pile the vegetables into our homemade wagon and go door-to-door selling the vegetables to our neighbors. At that early age, I learned I could earn more money selling than I could doing most other things and certainly more than working in the fields. While living in Gonzales most of my friends were Mexicans, so I learned most of the Mexican swear words at a very young age.

When I was eleven, our family moved to Salt Lake City, Utah, where I landed a job with the *Salt Lake City Tribune/Telegram,* selling newspaper subscriptions door-to-door.

When I was 12 or 13, I was hired to plant a field of corn for a Japanese neighbor. I was showed how to crawl down the row, dig a hole and place two kernels in each. I had to make sure not to plant it too shallow or too deep. If they were planted too close to the surface, the birds would eat them. The birds followed me through the field. The Japanese guy thought it would take me a week or so, he paid me by the day. I thought there must be a better way to do this. I went to a farm equipment store and asked what the best way was to plant corn. They had a special tool for planting corn. I couldn't afford to buy one. The guy at the store had an old one he gave for nothing. I still have it.

I planted the corn field using the corn planter. After filling the tube with corn kernels, I would push the point into the grown and release a couple of kernels. I finished the field in two days. The neighbor was very happy, and the corn grew and that made me happy. I had my corn planter out in my garden for the past 25 years and it was quite rusty. I painted it for this picture.

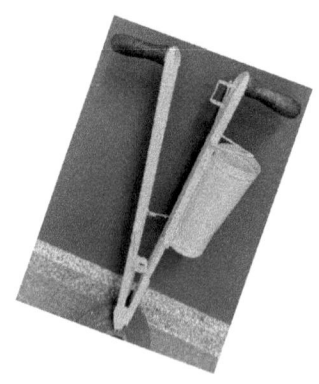

At the age of sixteen, still attending high school, I accepted a job selling, three-ply, stainless steel, waterless cookware to young girls for their HOPE chests. At the age of twenty-one, I began selling hearing aids, door-to-door, for Beltone Hearing Aid Company. While working for Beltone, I met Kenny Dahlberg. Kenny owned Dahlberg Hearing Aid Company. At the time, Beltone was the world's largest hearing aid manufacturer, and Dahlberg was second. Dahlberg Hearing Aid Company later changed its name to Miracle-Ear. I will tell you something important about Kenny Dahlberg a little later.

I started my life as a very poor person and yet was a millionaire by the time I was thirty-five. And that was back in the days when a million dollars was a lot of money.

"Here I am, I'm one of a kind.

A little bit different, than others you'll find!"

I'm an "Individual," meaning, I am not affiliated with any political or religious group. I believe when one joins a group, he or she gives up their independent thinking and no longer thinks for themselves. I have earned the right to be a "Free Agent!" Being a Free Agent gives me the FREEDOM of choice as an individual, not a member of a group. This is a FREEDOM I hold dear. I am not against Democrats, and I am not against Republicans. I believe in a two-or-more-party system of government. Early in my life, I was registered as a Democrat, as were my parents before me and their parents before them. Later, I became a Republican, and now I'm registered as Independent. I don't really care for that title because they refer to it as The Independent Party which makes me part of a group. I'm a little more independent than the Independent Party!

Independents often are portrayed as political free agents with the potential to alleviate the nation's rigid partisan divisions. Yet the reality is that most independents are not all that politically independent. The small share of Americans who are truly independent, have no partisan leaning, and that is my political position. I have found that after all is said and done there is a lot more said by politicians than is done. You will find me in the center only leaning in one direction or the other based on the issue or timely need. For example:

Pro-life vs. Pro-choice!

The pro-life and pro-choice labels are, at times, confusing for one main reason: They give people only two choices for all their religious, moral, political, and practical beliefs on abortion. Generally, people who identify as pro-choice believe that all women have the basic human right to decide when and whether to have children, even if you wouldn't choose abortion for yourself. One political party believes it is okay to abort babies, (pro-choice). When you say you're pro-choice, you're telling people that you believe it's okay for woman to have the ability to choose abortion as an option for an unplanned pregnancy. People who oppose abortion often call themselves "pro-life." This party believes you should not abort babies and upon conception, *that's a baby*.

On the other hand, if a person is in prison for raping and killing a young girl, the political party which believes it is okay to abort babies wants the convicted killer to be rehabilitated and then released. The party that believes you shouldn't abort babies believes in the death penalty and wants the convicted killer to be exterminated.

I don't believe it makes sense to use a "one size fits all" approach when deciding on a life. I believe that circumstances do matter, and it makes sense to make this important decision based upon the facts involved in each individual case. Irrespective of their stand on the pro-choice, pro-life issue, the parent or grandparent of the fourteen-year-old child who becomes pregnant by an undesirable will probably favor an abortion. And the parent or grandparent of the teen aged girl who was raped and killed, regardless of their stand on this issue, will probably favor the death penalty. A major difference between the two is that the unborn baby has committed no crime. I believe this weighty decision can only be made by those involved, based on the circumstances, and adoption may be the better choice.

As a child, I was a member of the organized religion of my parents. I believed then and still believe now there are many wonderful people who are followers of that religion. However, when I personally found I didn't believe what they were teaching, I quit!

I now belong to what I believe is the only

TRUE RELIGION!

I describe true religion as, "Whatever a person does religiously!" It's the day-by-day life one lives, not what is agreed upon one day a week. There is only one member in my church and that person is me. The decisions of how I live my life are mine, and your decisions are yours. You are either a good or a bad person, and that choice is yours. I believe what we do in our life, day by day is our true religion.

Living my life in the "Land of the Free and the Home of the Brave" has taught me a great deal about America and its people. Being raised as a poor minority in both a Black and Mexican community gave me a good perspective about a lot of things. Most Americans, irrespective of their color or race, are great people! If you are in need, Americans will be there for you! If you are hit by a natural disaster, Americans will send money and aid to help you out. If you need American sons and daughters to leave the comfort of home and risk their lives to fight for your freedom, they will be there for you. Americans love to see others succeed, they are kind and nice and, in my opinion, **most Americans are not racist.** I have traveled extensively and found that there are many beautiful countries and wonderful people in the world, but none is better than America and the American people.

Tell me where you've been, and,

I'll tell you where you are going!

Over time People change, and as they do, their culture changes, and as it does, their society changes, and then their nation changes.

Change is the price we must pay for progress!

All change, however, does not end with progress. All too often, change takes us sideways or backwards. Looking forward to change is positive only if you know where it is you want to go. Think about yourself, a citizen of your nation, as a boat out in the ocean. If what you plan for is "a calm, no problem existence," no matter which way the wind blows, it will rock your boat. If you know where you want to go, occasionally you will find yourself in the middle of a favorable wind that will move you, towards that which you desire at an unbelievable speed. In this book we will analyze our selected leaders to determine what they have done to move us towards America's most precious possession, which is . . .

FREEDOM for all Americans!

As you read about each leader, ask yourself if you think he was a good or great president, and would you have voted for him? Don't consider his political affiliation, just his accomplishments. I have found, *"There is some good in the bad ones, and some bad in the good ones."*

CHAPTER TWO

Calvin Coolidge

Calvin Coolidge

W̲e will begin our quest one hundred years ago. The president of the United States from 1923 to 1929 was **John Calvin Coolidge, Jr**. Coolidge was the thirtieth president of the United States.

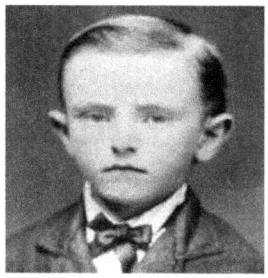

Calvin

Coolidge was born on a farm in Vermont on the Fourth of July in 1872. Calvin, as he was called, grew up doing daily chores and selling apples. Calvin's father was a successful farmer and storekeeper. Later, his father served in the Vermont House of Representatives and the Senate. Calvin was close to his father and accompanied him while he was engaged in his many occupations. Calvin observed that his father was an incredibly quiet man of few words. Calvin saw his dad's silence as a strong negotiation strategy. When someone made Calvin's father an offer, he would just sit and wait silently; he then usually received a better offer. Calvin modeled himself after his father and became known as, "Silent Cal." To say the least, Silent Cal's press conferences were a joke. Here is one from his 1924 political campaign: Reporter; *"Have you any Statement from the campaign?"* Silent Cal: *"No." "Can you tell us something about the world situation?"* Silent Cal: *"No." "Any information about prohibition?"* Silent Cal: *"No."*

And the best part, Silent Cal said, *"Please don't quote me!"*

Helen Keller with Grace Coolidge

Coolidge married Grace Anna Goodhue on October 4, 1905. Grace was a teacher at the Clarke Institute for the Deaf in Northampton, MA. Calvin first caught her attention when she saw him through an open window of the boardinghouse where he lived. There he was, standing in his underwear and wearing a derby hat while shaving. She laughed loud enough for him to hear her. His short marriage proposal was, "I'm going to be married to you." Grace fell in love with his short, rather blunt approach. As the First Lady, Grace, being educated and working with the deaf, sought out people with disabilities to visit the White House. **Helen Keller** was a favorite. Helen Keller lost her sight and hearing after a bout of scarlet fever at the age of nineteen months. She became the first deaf and blind person to earn a Bachelor of Arts degree. She often commented that the loss of hearing was worse than the loss of sight. She once said,

> *"When you lose your sight, you lose contact with things. When you lose your hearing, you lose contact with people!"*

This is a funny story that was often repeated during the Coolidge presidency:

> *One day, the president and Mrs. Coolidge were visiting a government farm. Soon after their arrival, they were taken off on separate tours. When Mrs. Coolidge passed the chicken pens, she paused to ask the man in charge if the rooster copulates more than once a day. "Dozens of times," was the reply. "Please tell that to the president," Mrs. Coolidge requested. When the president passed the pens and was told about the rooster, he asked "Same hen every time?" "Oh no, Mr. President, a different one each time." The president nodded slowly, then said, "Tell that to the First Lady."*

The biological sensation of men's re-arousal by the presence of an unknown new female is today called the "Coolidge effect," *named after President Coolidge.* While my research has not uncovered any extra marital relationships, Coolidge was often referred to as, "Silent, Sexy Cal!"

A socialite after meeting Coolidge said,

> "A friend of mine bet me I couldn't get you to say three words!" Silent Cal answered as he walked away,

> "You lose!"

Coolidge also said,

> "The things I don't say, never get me into trouble."

And

> "No one ever lost their job by listening too much!"

Coolidge, an intelligent man with an estimated IQ of 127 once said of himself, "I am hard to get along with!"

Both Coolidge's mother and younger sister died while he was a teenager. His father then married a local schoolteacher in 1891. Calvin went to Amherst College which was, at the time, an all-male school where students who consumed alcohol or played cards were subject to expulsion. Coolidge had a reputation on campus for his dry wit and his public speaking. Later in life, philosophizing on the purpose of education, he would say,

> "Education is to teach men not what to think,
>
> but how to think."

After graduating Cum Laude from Amherst, Calvin took an apprenticeship with a local law office.

Calvin then began a quiet climb up the political ladder, as mayor of Northampton, as a state congressman, serving in the Massachusetts House of Representatives, as a state senator, and as lieutenant governor. During this period, Coolidge studied public policy questions, made speeches, and steadily gained influence with Republican Party leaders. He developed a reputation as a pro-business conservative who strove to make government lean and efficient. In 1918, Coolidge was elected governor of Massachusetts.

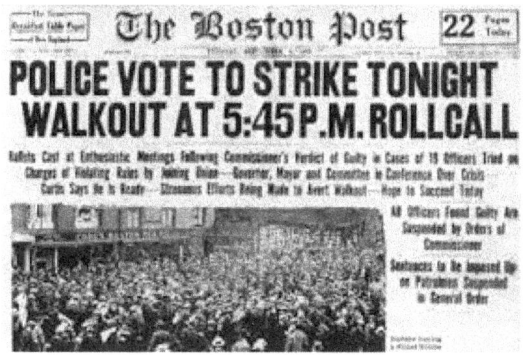

The "Great Boston Police Strike of 1919." The Boston City Police wanted to unionize and called a strike. Chaos and looting erupted in the un-policed streets of Boston. Calvin stood his ground; he called in the National Guard to restore order and fired all striking officers. Coolidge barred the police from returning to their jobs. He declared,

"There is no right to strike against public safety by anybody, anywhere, anytime."

The American public was appalled by violence in the streets of Boston and felt like the police had abandoned them. So, when Coolidge went on the attack rather than strike a deal, he became a national hero. (Years later **President Ronald Reagan** copied this approach to solve the air traffic controller's strike. Coolidge was one of Reagan's favorite former presidents.)

The Republican party impressed by Calvin's popularity named him as the running mate to presidential candidate, Warren Harding. Harding and Coolidge beat James M. Cox and vice-president hopeful Franklin D. Roosevelt by a landslide making Coolidge the only person to ever defeat Roosevelt in a national election. Harding's presidency was referred to as the **"Cavalcade of Scandals."** His presidency was one of corruption and fraud. In 1922, Albert B. Fall, then secretary of the interior, leased the US Navy's **Teapot Dome** oil reserve near Casper, Wyoming, to the Mammoth Oil Company, which had been set up by Harry F. Sinclair. The lease was given without competitive bidding, and it granted Sinclair exclusive rights to take and dispose of all oil and gas from the reserve. It was later disclosed that Fall had received large cash gifts and "no-interest loans" from Sinclair. At the time, this was the biggest government scandal ever in political history. By the time of his retirement in 1949, Sinclair Oil was said to have assets of $1.2 billion, with yearly earnings of $68 million. In 1969, it was merged into Atlantic Richfield

Company. Harding also stole life-saving medicine from veteran's hospitals.

Warren G Harding

During Prohibition you were legally allowed to consume any alcohol already in your possession. It was said that Harding ran the White House like a speakeasy. During one drunken party Harding lost the White House chinaware in a poker game.

Harding had the first radio installed in the White House in 1922.

Florence Kling   **Carrie Phillips**

He married **Florence Kling** on July 8, 1891. Harding is reported to have had an affair for fifteen years with **Carrie Fulton Phillips**, the wife of one of Harding's friends, James Phillips, before Harding became president. Carrie threatened to expose the affair if she wasn't paid for her silence. With the fear of a scandal prior to the election, the Republican National Committee paid her fifty thousand dollars, an enormous amount at the time. She also received monthly payments of five thousand dollars. Harding wrote poetry letters to Carrie during their illicit affair. In 1968, those letters were brought forward.

Nan and Liz

Before becoming president, Harding began a relationship with **Nan Britton**. Nan was thirty years younger than Warren. It was rumored that he had sexual liaisons with her in the White House. In a book she authored in 1927, she claimed to have given birth to Harding's daughter, Elizabeth Ann. Harding's DNA has since confirmed Elizabeth Ann was his daughter. Warren Harding is remembered as one of the ineptest presidents in United States history. However, the most scandalous part of this scandalous tale is the questions associated with Harding's untimely death in 1923. While stopping over in San Francisco from a trip to Alaska and Canada, he came down with ptomaine poisoning (food poisoning) contracted from tainted Japanese crabmeat and died. Rumors circulated widely that his wife, Florence, poisoned him, since she declined an autopsy and had him embalmed one hour later. Official records state he died of a heart attack. Harding's presidency was over one hundred years ago, and I mention it only because he was Coolidge's predecessor.

Calvin was vacationing at his father's farm in Plymouth, Vermont, when word of Harding's death arrived by messenger (his father's home did not have electricity or a telephone). At 2:47 a.m. on August 2, 1923, Coolidge changed out of his pajamas into a black suit to be sworn in, with his hand on the family Bible, by his own father, as the thirtieth president of the

United States. Calvin's father was a notary public. Calvin then went back to bed. Calvin was fifty-one years old at the time. As President, Calvin was known to do a lot of sleeping.

Coolidge had an image of being honest and <u>not</u> susceptible to corruption, so Harding never involved Coolidge in on his corrupt money-making. Coolidge gave a positive light to the White House following the dark misdoings from the Harding era. Coolidge took Harding's corruption straight on just like the Boston Police Strike and did away with all of Harding's cronies.

During the Coolidge presidency, the White House was turned into a veritable animal menagerie. Calvin and Grace loved animals, both wild and domesticated. Once the public got wind, many kinds of animals were gifted to them. Such as a pygmy hippo named Billy and two lion cubs named "Tax Reduction" and "Budget Bureau."

In 1924 Coolidge signed into law a measure guaranteeing full American citizenship for all Native Americans born within US territorial limits.

Also in 1924, Coolidge sought reelection and carried over 54 percent of the vote with the slogan *"Keep Cool with Coolidge."*

He won by the largest popularity than any president up until that time.

Coolidge stated at his Inaugural Address, March 4, 1925:

> *I favor the policy of economy, not because I wish to save money, but because I wish to save people. The men and women of this country who toil are the ones who bear the cost of the Government. Every dollar that we carelessly waste means that their life will be so much more meager. Every dollar that we prudently save means that their life will be so much more abundant. Economy is idealism in its most practical form.*

Silent Cal believed that tax cuts for the wealthiest Americans would benefit all Americans. He lowered income taxes and all other taxes that were necessary during WWI. Coolidge was correct; the tax cuts encouraged wealthy Americans to invest more money into business improvements and the economy grew rapidly. Calvin's approach will be copied by many presidents of the future including John Kennedy, Ronald Reagan, and Donald Trump. It worked well each time it was copied.

The strong economy combined with restrained government spending produced consistent government surpluses that caused the total federal debt to shrink by one quarter during Coolidge's presidency. He was one of the few presidents to run a budget surplus. As he put it,

> "Collecting more taxes than is absolutely necessary is legalized robbery."

Coolidge's presidency was the age of the **Roaring Twenties**! It was the era of prohibition, speakeasies, jazz music, the arrival of big-time movie stars. To name a few, Charlie Chaplin, John Barrymore, Joan Crawford, Louis Armstrong, and Bing Crosby.

The **Roarin' Twenties** were *a* time of growth, strong wages, and very little unemployment. The automotive industry, the film industry, the radio industry, and the chemical industry took off during the twenties.

With the passage of the 19th Amendment in 1920 that gave women the right to vote, American feminists attained political equality.

The Flapper

A new woman was born, and she was called a "flapper" who danced, drank, smoked, and voted.

This new woman cut her hair, wore make-up, and partied. She was known for being giddy and taking risks. The back seat of a car became a great place for necking.

In 1925 electrical recording, one of the greater advances in sound recording, brought about gramophone records. The introduction of sound film, "the talkies" didn't surge until later in the 1920s.

Lindbergh & the Spirit of St. Louis

In 1927 Charles Lindberg rose to fame with the first solo nonstop transatlantic flight. He took off from Roosevelt Field in New York and landed at Paris, Le Bourget Airport. It took Lindbergh 33.5 hours to cross the Atlantic Ocean. His aircraft, the Spirit of St. Louis, was a custom-built, single engine, single-seat monoplane.

On October 6, 1927, the first "talkie," *The Jazz Singer*, starring Al Jolson, debuts. I remember him singing "Mammy" in "Blackface."

In 1928 the Walt Disney cartoon character "Micky Mouse" made his debut in a silent animated short "Plane Crazy." Mickey made his debut in a "talkie" as "Steamboat Willie" on November 18, 1928.

Steamboat Willie

Homosexuality became much more visible and somewhat more acceptable. One popular American song, "Masculine Women, Feminine Men," was released in 1926 and recorded by numerous artists of the day; it included these lyrics:

Masculine women, Feminine men,
Which is the rooster, which is the hen?
It's hard to tell 'em apart today! And, say!
Sister is busy learning to shave,
Brother just loves his permanent wave,
It's hard to tell 'em apart today! Hey, hey!
Girls were girls and boys were boys when I was a tot,
Now we don't know who is who, or even what's what!
Knickers and trousers, baggy and wide,
Nobody knows who's walking inside,
Those masculine women and feminine men!

Speakeasies were illegal bars selling beer and liquor after paying off local police and government officials. They became popular in major cities and helped fund large-scale gangsters' operations such as those of Lucky Luciano, Al Capone, Meyer Lansky, and Ben Siegel. They operated with connections to organized crime and liquor smuggling. Benjamin "Bugsy" Siegel was an American mobster who was a driving force behind the development of the Las Vegas Strip financed by Mormon bankers, Jimmy Hoffa, and the Teamsters Union.

In 1924 **John Edgar Hoover** (not related to President Herbert Hoover) became the director of the FBI, Federal Bureau of Investigation. J. Edgar Hoover was one of the worst racist, misogynist, and greatest bigots to have ever been an FBI director. He considered Blacks inferior and "not good enough" to be FBI agents. Upon assuming the office of the director of the FBI, he fired all female agents from the bureau and made it impossible for women to be agents of the FBI; he considered women to be "pinheads." He was racially prejudiced. He shrugged off the miseries of black Americans, preferring to claim they were outside his jurisdiction. "I'm not going to send the FBI in," a Justice Department official recalled him saying testily, "every time some 'n-word' woman says she's been raped."

J. Edgar Hoover

Early in his career, Hoover helped popularize the federal "G-Man" as a gun-toting avenger going after bank robbers, kidnappers, and leftist labor agitators. Hoover used his considerable influence in Hollywood to ensure his agency was almost always portrayed in flattering ways.

His successes included the highly publicized killing of bank robber John Dillinger and other high-profile shootouts.

Hoover was feared by all politicians of the United States. He held president's hostage by having damming evidence against them. He kept records of all politicians' wrongdoing to use them as blackmail later. His strong hold on the politicians saw him lead the FBI for forty-eight years, through the terms of eight presidents from 1924 to 1972 when he finally died from a heart attack. It was widely known that John Edgar was a homosexual cross-dresser.

Due to Hoover's long stay in office, the US senate finally set the term limits on the FBI director to a single term of ten years.

About J. Edgar Hoover in private, on hearing that he had died, then President Richard M. Nixon had responded merely, *"Jesus Christ! That old cocksucker!"*

The most popular American athlete of the 1920s was baseball player Babe Ruth. Fans were enthralled in 1927 when Ruth hit sixty home runs, setting a new single-season home run record that was not broken until 1961.

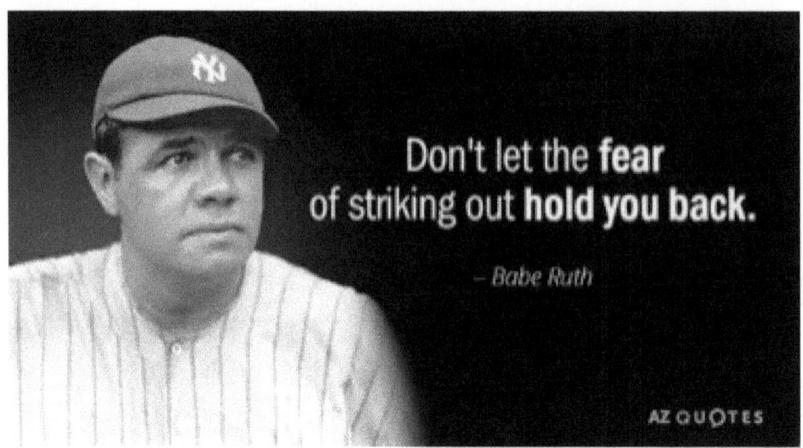

In the second half of the roaring twenties, Wall Street was doing a terrible job of regulating itself and was out of control. Inside trading was legal and was used to amass a fortune for a few wealthy men including Joseph P. Kennedy.

On June 30, 1924, Coolidge assembled his family for a few photographs. After picture taking at the White House, the two Coolidge sons, John and Calvin Jr. played several games of tennis. Calvin Jr. wore a blister on his toe from wearing tennis shoes without socks. The blister became infected and led to severe blood poisoning. With no antibody to cure the infection, at sixteen years old, Calvin Coolidge, Jr. died. With the death of his son, Coolidge's need for sleep became extreme. His midday naps often lasted from lunch until dinner. He usually slept eleven hours nightly. At the time, rumors claimed that the First Lady had intimate liaisons with secret service agents. However, it was never proven.

With a failing economy, Coolidge decided not to run for office again. On August 2, 1927, while vacationing in South

Dakota, Coolidge beckoned reporters to an impromptu press conference and handed them a slip of paper that stated, "I do not choose to run for president in 1928." Coolidge answered "No" to any questions. A concise conclusion to a concise presidency.

Calvin Coolidge died of a heart attack on January 5, 1933.

CHAPTER THREE

Herbert Hoover

Herbert Hoover

The thirty-first president of the United States was Republican, **Herbert Clark Hoover** from 1929 to 1932.

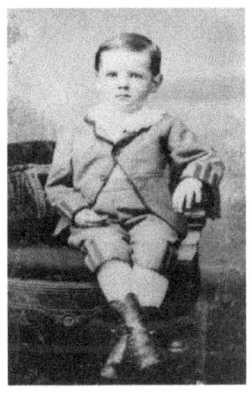

Herbert

Hoover was born on August 10, 1874, in West Branch, Iowa, the first president born west of the Mississippi. His father, Jesse Hoover, was a blacksmith and owned a store that sold farm equipment. The family were Quakers. Around age two "Bertie," as he was called during that time, contracted a serious bout of respiratory infection, and was momentarily thought to have died until resuscitated by his uncle, Dr. John Minthorn. As a young child he was often referred to by his father as "my little stick in the mud" when he repeatedly got trapped in the mud crossing the unpaved street. Herbert's father died in 1880 at the age of thirty-four from a heart attack when Herbert was just six years old. Three years later, his mother died of pneumonia, orphaning Herbert who was only nine years old. After being passed around to different family members, Herbert's uncle,

Dr. John Minthorn had Herbert put on a train and sent two thousand miles away to Oregon to live with him and his wife after the loss of their own son. Their home was not a warm one as they were deeply religious, and he was raised in a strict Quaker household. Even though Hoover's IQ was estimated at 130, he only excelled at math, but overall, he was a very poor student. The Minthorn household was considered cultured and educational, and instilled a strong work ethic in Herbert. Herbert attended the newly established Stanford University in California. While at the university, he was the student manager of both the baseball and football teams and was a part of the inaugural Big Game versus rival the University of California and Stanford won.

Lou Henry Hoover

After graduating from Stanford with a degree in geology, Herbert became a mining engineer, traveling the world to evaluate prospective mines for potential purchase. Herbert made a promise to a classmate who was the only female geology student at Stanford, that he would marry her when he returned from his trip to Australia. True to his word, he sent Lou Henry a telegram and proposed. Upon his return in 1899, they were married, and she accompanied Herbert in his travels. Lou quickly mastered eight languages in their travels. Later, the First Lady and the President would often speak Mandarin when they wanted to avoid being overheard by the White House staff. By 1914, Hoover was a wealthy man, with an estimated personal fortune of four million dollars. Worth over one hundred million in today's money. Hoover was once quoted as saying,

> "If a man has not made a million dollars by the time, he is forty, he is not worth much."

Hoover worked fourteen-hour days and secured his wealth from high-salaried positions, his ownership of profitable Burmese silver mines, and royalties from writing the leading textbook on mining engineering.

At the start of World War I in 1914, Hoover dedicated his talents to humanitarian work. He helped 120,000 stranded American tourists return home from Europe when the hostilities broke out. He coordinated the delivery of food and supplies to citizens of Belgium after that country was overrun by Germany. Hoover was known as the "Great Humanitarian." Hoover liked to say that the difference between dictatorship and democracy was simple,

> "Dictators organize from the top down, democracies from the bottom up."

Winston Churchill, who Hoover intensely disliked considered Hoover a stubborn "son of a bitch."

In his years after the war, Hoover became the director general of the American Relief Administration, an agency established to address the widespread famine in Europe. As a result of his humanitarianism, he was widely admired in the United States and sought by both political parties as a candidate for president in 1920.

Hoover eventually declared himself a Republican and accepted President Warren Harding's invitation to serve as Secretary of Commerce. At the Department of Commerce, where he served through both the Harding and Coolidge administrations, he established a wide range of standards for manufactured products, campaigned against waste and inefficiency in industry, and encouraged the growth of new industries such as radio and aviation. He became one of the most admired men in Washington, but his fame reached new heights in 1927 because of his extraordinary service to assist the victims of the Mississippi River Flood that year.

His "Own Your Own Home" campaign was a collaboration to promote ownership of single-family dwellings, with groups such as the Better Houses in America movement, the Architects' Small House Service Bureau, and the Home Modernizing Bureau. He worked with bankers and the savings and loan industry to promote the new "long-term home mortgages," which dramatically stimulated home construction. Hoover wanted the long-term home mortgage loan to be available to all Americans, so all could prosper. That changed with the next president when he made these loans unattainable to black people during redlining. Redlining caused a wide financial gap between White and Black Americans.

Although Hoover continued to consider Harding ill-suited to be president, the two men nevertheless became friends. Hoover accompanied Harding on his final trip out West in 1923. It was Hoover who called for a specialist to tend to the ailing chief executive, and it was also Hoover who contacted the White House to inform them of the president's death.

Coolidge had been reluctant to choose Hoover as his successor; on one occasion he remarked that, "For six years Hoover has given me unsolicited advice, all of it bad." I was particularly offended when he commented to me,

"Shit or get off the pot!"

On November 19, 1928, President-elect Hoover embarked on a ten-nation "goodwill tour" of Central and South America. While crossing the Andes Mountains from Chile, an assassination plot by Argentine anarchists was thwarted. The group was led by Severino Di Giovanni, who planned to blow up his train as it crossed the Argentinian central plain. The plotters had an itinerary, but the bomber was arrested before he could place the explosives on the rails. Hoover professed unconcern, tearing off the front page of a newspaper that revealed the plot and explaining, "It's just as well that Lou shouldn't see it." His complimentary remarks on Argentina were well received in both the host country and in the press.

Di Giovanni

When President Coolidge chose not to run for another term, Hoover easily won the Republican nomination despite never having held an elected office. He defeated Alfred E. Smith, the Democratic governor of New York, in a landslide.

Hoover declared in his inaugural address,

> "I have no fears for the future of our country,
>
> It is bright with hope."

Hoover, who had made a small fortune in mining, was the first president to redistribute his salary and donated all his paychecks to charity.

Just seven months into his presidency on October 29, 1929, known as Black Tuesday, the stock market lost 90 percent of its value. During the next four years eleven thousand banks failed leaving many Americans with no savings. Average income dropped by 40 percent. Unemployment was 3 percent in 1929 and fell to 25 percent by 1933. Hoover bore much of the blame in the minds of the American people for the Great Depression.

Newspapers were called "Hoover blankets" and "Hoover Pullmans" were boxcars, in which two hundred thousand starving Americans rode all over the country pursuing jobs.

Hoover established set days for people to avoid eating specified foods and save them for soldiers' rations: meatless Mondays, wheatless Wednesdays, and

"When in doubt, eat potatoes."

Hoover had a bizarre relationship with White House staff. First Lady Lou Hoover communicated with staff via sign language for efficiency. An example would be touching her hair which meant dinner for guests was to be announced.

Hoover paid for the first Presidential Summer Camp in 1932. He spent many hours fishing and entertaining dignitaries at the camp. He later donated the camp (referred to as "the Brown House") to the Commonwealth of Virginia when he left office.

Hoover avoided all interactions with servants and desired to not even see them. The White House bell system was used to coordinate the distance between him and people who serviced him. Three rings announced his approach, requiring staff to hide in the nearest closet until he was out of sight. Same with the groundskeepers who found themselves jumping behind bushes when he was rumored to be in proximity. His public image was rigid and officious (he even wore a tie fishing.) Lunch and dinner required formal attire with most meals offering seven courses. The White House lived like aristocracy. A lavish lifestyle was a bad look while the rest of the nation wallowed in deprivation.

Hoover Dam

Hoover tried to combat the ensuing Great Depression with government enforced efforts and **public works projects** such as the Hoover Dam. These initiatives did not produce economic recovery during his term but served as the groundwork for various policies incorporated in Franklin D. Roosevelt's New Deal including the Works Progress Administration (WPA).

The consensus among historians is that Hoover's defeat in the 1932 election was caused primarily by his failure to end the downward economic spiral, along with his support for strong enforcement of prohibition. He began to feel sorry for himself. His hair went gray, he lost over thirty-five pounds, and his mood turned dismal. Hoover's domestic policy achievements include unprecedented prison reform, concentration on child health and protection, and the establishment of the Reconstruction Finance Corporation (RFC). In foreign affairs, his Good Neighbor policy improved US relations with Latin American nations.

Herbert Hoover

The president's political reputation plummeted with the rising unemployment. By 1932 unemployment had reached 24.9 percent, businesses defaulted on record numbers of loans, and more than five thousand banks had failed. Hundreds of thousands of Americans found themselves homeless and began congregating what became known as Hooverville's. Hooverville's were "shanty towns" that sprang up in major cities. New Dealer Rexford Tugwell who served in FDR's first "Brain Trust," a group of Columbia University academics who made recommendations on Roosevelt's New Deal programs, remarked that although no one would say so at the time, "practically the whole New Deal was extrapolated from programs that Hoover started."

A Hooverville

Hoover mounted a vigorous campaign for re-election in 1932 and traveled the country by train, defending his policies at every stop. But it came as no surprise to Hoover that he lost to Franklin D. Roosevelt in the general election.

A few Hoover quotes:

"No man in public can be just a little crooked."

"Blessed are the young for they shall inherit the national debt."

"Older men declare war, but it's the youth that must fight and die."

Hoover died following massive internal bleeding at the age of ninety in his New York City suite at 11:35 a.m. on October 20, 1964, thirty-one years, seven months, and sixteen days after leaving office. At the time of his death, he had the longest retirement of any president.

CHAPTER FOUR

Franklin Delano Roosevelt

The Hoover Dam was constructed between 1931 and 1936 during the Great Depression and was dedicated on September 30, 1935, by **President Franklin D. Roosevelt.** Its construction was the result of a massive effort involving thousands of workers, and cost over one hundred lives. Democrat Roosevelt did not like Republican Hoover's name on the dam and renamed it Boulder Dam. The Hoover Dam name was restored by Congress in 1947.

On February 15, 1933, just over two weeks before Franklin D. Roosevelt was inaugurated as president of the United States, Roosevelt arrived at the Bayfront Park in Miami, Florida around 9:00 p.m. to give a speech from the back seat of his light-blue open touring car.

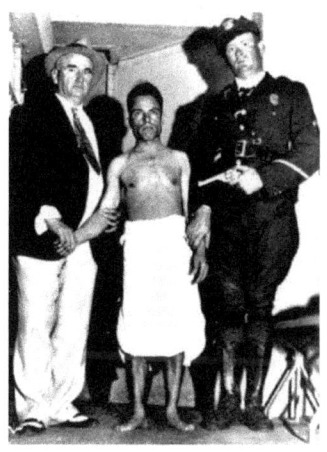

"Little Joe"

After a thirty-five minute speech he was talking to supporters who had gathered around his car, when five shots rang out. Giuseppe "Joe" Zangara, a deranged unemployed bricklayer, emptied the thirty-two-caliber pistol he had purchased for eight dollars, at Roosevelt. Zangara, an Italian immigrant, shouted out, "Too many people are starving" as he fired his gun.

Zangara was close enough to kill Roosevelt, about twenty to twenty-five feet away. However, since Zangara was very short, only 5'1", he wasn't tall enough see Roosevelt, so he climbed up on a wobbly chair to look over the crowd. A woman named Lillian Cross, who stood near Zangara, claimed she hit Zangara's hand with her purse during the shooting. Joe Zangara was caught immediately and taken into custody.

Whether it was because of bad aim, the wobbly chair, or Mrs. Cross's intervention, all five bullets missed Roosevelt. Five bystanders were hit. Four received minor injuries; Chicago's Mayor **Anton Cermak** received a mortal shot to the lung in the attack. Several men tackled the assailant and might have beaten him to death if Roosevelt had not intervened, telling the crowd to leave justice to the authorities.

During the whole ordeal, Roosevelt was calm, brave, and decisive. Roosevelt's driver wanted to rush the president-elect to safety, but Roosevelt ordered the car to stop and pick up the wounded. On their way to the hospital, Roosevelt cradled Cermak's head on his shoulder, offering calming and comforting words which doctors later reported kept Cermak from going into shock. At the hospital Cermak whispered to Roosevelt, "I'm glad it was me and not you." His whispered comment is etched on Cermak's tombstone. Roosevelt spent several hours at the hospital, visiting each of the wounded. He came back the following day to check on them again.

The United States needed a strong leader; the untested president-elect proved himself strong and reliable in the face of crisis. Newspapers reported on both Roosevelt's actions and demeanor, putting faith in Roosevelt before he even stepped into office.

When Cermak died of his wounds on March 6, 1933, Zangara was charged with first-degree murder and sentenced to death. Zangara pleaded guilty. Zangara said in court, "No point living. Give me electric chair." On March 20, 1933, Zangara strode to the electric chair unaided and then plunked himself down. His last words were,

"Pusha da button!"

Going back a little, Roosevelt won the election to the New York Senate in 1910. Franklin was the fifth cousin of Theodore "Teddy" Roosevelt whom he greatly admired even though he was a Republican. Teddy Roosevelt was the twenty-sixth president from 1901 to 1909. President Wilson appointed Franklin as the assistant secretary of the navy, and he was the Democratic nominee for vice president in 1920.

On St. Patrick's Day 1905, Franklin married his fifth cousin once removed, Eleanor. Eleanor's father was deceased so her uncle, Teddy gave the bride away. Eleanor gave birth to six children of whom five survived into adulthood.

Eleanor

Eleanor found love letters in Franklin's suitcase revealing an affair Franklin was having with Lucy Mercer in 1918.

Lucy Mercer

Eleanor asked for a divorce. Franklin's mother, Sara said, "There's never been a divorce in the Roosevelt family and it won't start now." She demanded Franklin and Eleanor stay married or they would both lose their inheritance. Sara agreed to support them only if they remained married. Eleanor agreed with two conditions: one, Franklin could never again see Lucy, and two, she and Franklin would never again sleep in the same bed. Franklin promised never to see Lucy again, a promise he never kept. Lucy Mercer was Eleanor's social secretary. Lucy was a tall and beautiful young woman with thick blonde hair.

Eleanor explained to her daughter that she didn't sleep with Franklin because she did not like having sex with him. Roosevelt had several extramarital affairs, including the one he continued with Lucy Mercer, which began in 1914 and ended when he died. Lucy was the love of Franklin's life.

Eleanor spent her time with women who were known to be lesbians, and she exchanged thousands of steamy letters with close "friend" reporter Lorena Hickock. Hickock was an accomplished woman in her own right. She was a boundary-breaking reporter at the top of her field covering news, politics, and sports. Nicknamed "Hick" to Roosevelt and all her friends, Hickock was the first woman to have her byline featured on the front page of the New York Times. Like the other women in Eleanor's life, Hick was known to be a lesbian.

Hickock and Roosevelt first crossed paths when Hickock was assigned to interview the future First Lady in 1932 during FDR's first presidential campaign. By the following year, they were spending almost every day together. They became so close that Hickock could no longer cover the Roosevelts objectively; instead, she got a job as a researcher for FDR's New Deal initiative. She moved into the White House, in a bedroom conjoining Eleanor's. Eleanor's outward involvement with women caused an acceptance of Franklin's affairs with a number of other women.

Eleanor and Hick

The Roosevelt marriage from 1918 on was more of a political partnership. Eleanor described their relationship as "Together but separate!" Eleanor moved into her own house and never again lived with the president. She increasingly devoted herself to various charities and political causes independently of the president. She was a revolutionary first lady, one of the most ambitious and outspoken women to ever live in the White House. Although she was both criticized and praised for her active role in public policy, she is remembered as a humanitarian who dedicated much of her life to fighting for political and social change, and as one of the first public officials to publicize important issues through the mass media.

Eleanor had a loss of hearing and in 1955 was fitted with a set of the very first *eyeglass* hearing aids manufactured by Otarion. It was called "the Listener," and it took both eyeglass temples to house the hearing aid components. They were large and cumbersome to wear and added at least ten years to

Eleanor's appearance. As a result of her hearing loss, she became a proponent for better hearing with the use of amplification.

Eleanor Roosevelt

Eleanor Roosevelt was quoted as saying the following:

"A woman is like a tea bag; you never know how strong it is until it's in hot water."

"Yesterday is history. Tomorrow is a mystery. And today? Today is a gift."

Franklin's biggest personal hurdle was not his broken marriage, his biggest challenge came in the summer of 1921 at the age of thirty-nine. After swimming in the waters, while vacationing at Campobello Island, New Brunswick, Canada, he was diagnosed with a crippling disease that left him paralyzed from the waist down. Franklin was thought to have polio. For the rest of his life, he used a cane and metal braces to stand and walk short distances. When he was not in public, he moved around in a wheelchair. Roosevelt feared that a man in a wheelchair would be seen as "half a man," weak, and unable to provide strong leadership. He was careful to never be seen in public using a wheelchair, and had a car modified so that he could drive using only his hands, though that meant bracing the steering wheel with only his torso while he used both hands to work the other controls. He'd often end a conversation by smiling and saying, "Gotta run!"

In his campaign for president, Roosevelt placed blame for the beginning of the Great Depression on his opponent, President Herbert Hoover. He called it "Hoover's Depression." Roosevelt declared of Hoover:

"There is nothing inside the man but jelly!"

It is apparent that most of the presidents took credit for everything their predecessor did that was good and blamed all that was bad on his predecessor, especially if his predecessor was from the opposing party.

Joseph Stalin

As the story goes, Russia's Joseph Stalin on his death bed and, knowing that his time was short, and that Nikita Khrushchev would be his eventual successor, summoned Nikita to a very private meeting. After telling Khrushchev how lonely it could get at the top, Stalin said: "I've left for you two letters containing my wisest counsel in the bottom drawer of the desk. Do not open the first one until things are totally terrible. The second letter should only be opened when you are sure there are no answers to your problems, when you are despairing."

Khrushchev

Khrushchev took over and enjoyed a Russian honeymoon. Then followed trouble: a failed harvest; the five-year plan was two years late and many rubles short; and plotting by his political enemies. At 3:00 a.m. one morning, Khrushchev broke down and opened the bottom desk drawer and read the first letter.

Its message: "Blame everything on me, Stalin."

That's what Khrushchev did successfully in a major party address. All the troubles of the present were pinned on the policies of his predecessor. It worked, and the pressure was off, for a while.

The second honeymoon was brief. Hostilities along the Chinese border, another lousy crop and the humiliating Cuban missile crisis did very little for Khrushchev's job rating and even less for his own peace of mind. He was down. Then he remembered the bottom desk drawer. Making certain he was alone, Khrushchev quietly opened the envelope and read the one-line message:

"Write two letters, Stalin."

Franklin D. Roosevelt a Democrat became the thirty-second president of the United States, from 1933 to 1945.

Franklin D. Roosevelt

Roosevelt was elected president in November 1932, in the depth of the Great Depression. Roosevelt was still struggling with his own physical disability, as he helped the American people regain faith in themselves. He brought hope as he promised prompt, vigorous action, and asserted in his Inaugural Address,

"The only thing we have to fear is fear itself."

He confronted the Depression with the idea of: Try something, anything, and if it did not work, try something else. Franklin Delano Roosevelt, was often referred to by his initials **"FDR."** Many historians rank FDR along with George Washington and Abraham Lincoln, as the three greatest presidents.

Roosevelt's biographier, Jean Edward Smith in 2007 stated,

> "He lifted himself from a wheelchair to lift the nation from its knees."

For the first time in a long time Americans felt they had a president who was strong and caring. For the first time in a long time Americans felt they had a president who could bring them together. Americans felt they were not alone. They felt that America with Roosevelt was coming back! Americans believed that he would be their leader for a long, long time, and he was.

Franklin

Roosevelt was born January 30, 1882, in Hyde Park, New York. He grew up in a very wealthy family. As a child, he learned to sail, and when he was sixteen, his father gave him a sailboat. Due to many family trips to Europe, and because of private tutors, Roosevelt became conversant in German and French. He attended Harvard University and Columbia Law School. Roosevelt was an average student academically, and he later declared,

> "I took economics in college for four years, and everything I was taught was wrong."

Roosevelt, was the first US president to fly in an airplane.

FDR spoke to the American public daily through the radio, in what became known as "Fireside Chats." America was in the throes of the Great Depression when Roosevelt took office. Unemployment was over thirteen million and there was a run on the banks. The American public had lost faith in most financial institutions. Roosevelt immediately declared a national bank holiday, halting all banking operations in the United States. He explained his new banking policy in a fireside chat and Congress passed the "Emergency Banking Act," which restored faith in the banking institutions. The run on the banks halted. The FDIC, Federal Deposit Insurance Corporation was created, and it guaranteed individual accounts of up to five thousand dollars which gave depositors confidence that their savings were safe.

The rapid expansion of government programs that occurred during Roosevelt's term redefined the role of the government in the United States and Roosevelt's advocacy of government social programs was instrumental in redefining liberalism for coming generations.

On January 30, 1933, **Adolf Hitler** became chancellor of Germany, and then assumed the title of Führer und Reichskanzler in 1934 (Leader and Chancellor).

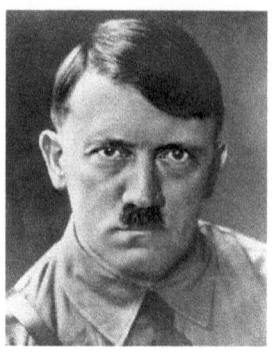

Adolf Hitler

The **Social Security Act of 1935** was signed into law by Roosevelt. The law created the Social Security program as well as insurance against unemployment. The Social Security program was designed in such a way that people would work for many years paying in taxes but would not live long enough to collect benefits. Life expectancy at birth in 1930 was indeed only fifty-eight for men and sixty-two for women, and the retirement age was sixty-five. Americans are living longer, and Social Security benefits are payable to over sixty-four million beneficiaries in January 2022.

In 1935, the unemployment rate was staggering. Roosevelt created the **WPA** (Work Projects Administration) which employed mostly unskilled men to carry out public works and infrastructure projects. They built more than four thousand new school buildings, erected 130 new hospitals, laid roughly 9,000 miles of storm drains and sanitary sewer lines, built 29,000 new bridges, constructed 150 new airfields, paved, or repaired 280,000 miles of roads, and planted 24 million trees. In 1935, the WPA employed approximately 350,000 Black Americans, about 15 percent of its total workforce. As a result, Roosevelt was viewed as a hero by many Black Americans.

In 1936, Roosevelt was re-elected by a top-heavy margin. Feeling he was armed with a popular mandate, he sought legislation to enlarge the United States Supreme Court, Titled Roosevelt's Court Packing Plan, which would have added six more members to the Supreme Court. Roosevelt's court packing plan failed; however, no president since George Washington selected more men to sit on the Supreme Court. They were all white men. The "liberal-conservative" make-up of the Supreme Court changes with each presidential appointment affecting the outcome of each decision the court makes and the balance of the Judicial branch.

A 1937 political cartoon with the caption, "We don't want a ventriloquist act in the Supreme Court!" depicting Roosevelt with five puppets

The Constitution of the United States divides the federal government into three branches to make sure no individual or group will have too much power:

- **Executive**—Carries out laws (president, vice president, cabinet, most federal agencies). The president can veto legislation created by Congress and nominates heads of federal agencies.

- **Legislative**—Makes laws (Congress, comprised of the House of Representatives with 435 members and the Senate with 100 members, two from each state.) Congress confirms or rejects the president's nominees and can remove the president from office in exceptional circumstances.

- **Judicial** — Evaluates laws (Supreme Court and other courts). The Justices of the Supreme Court, who can overturn unconstitutional laws, are nominated by the president, and confirmed by the Senate. Term is for life.

This ability of each branch to respond to the actions of the other two branches is called the system of checks and balances.

In 1938, FDR founded **The March of Dimes.**

Hitler's invasion of Poland in September 1939 drove Great Britain and France to declare war on Germany. Winston Churchill in 1940, watched with horror as the Nazis invaded and occupied France in a matter of weeks. Britain was now fighting Germany essentially on its own, and it seemed very possible that Adolf Hitler would win. In what's known as the "destroyers-for-bases deal," FDR traded the World War I-era destroyers in exchange for ninety-nine-year leases on some British bases in the Western Hemisphere.

On December 7, 1941, the Japanese waged a surprise attack on Pearl Harbor. Over 2,200 Americans died in the attack and on December 8, 1941, America entered the war.

Roosevelt made this announcement,

> "No matter how long it may take us to overcome this premediated invasion, the American people will win through to absolute victory."

Roosevelt was elected to a third and died during his fourth term, (1941-1945). WWII dominated FDR's attention. His administration oversaw the construction of the Pentagon.

The Pentagon is the world's largest office building, with about 6.5 million square feet.

The Pentagon

Roosevelt initiated the development of the world's first atomic bomb. He kept it secret, didn't even tell Truman, his vice-president. Feeling that world peace in the future would depend upon relations between the United States and Russia, he devoted much thought to the planning of a **United Nations**, in which, he hoped, international difficulties could be settled. It was under his wartime leadership that the United States would become a "superpower" on the world stage. When the war began, quickie marriages became the norm, as teenage girls married their sweethearts before their men went overseas. As the men fought abroad, women on the Home Front worked in defense plants and volunteered for war-related organizations, in addition to managing their households. In New Orleans, as the demand for public transportation grew, women even became streetcar "conductorettes" for the first time. When men left, women became proficient cooks and housekeepers, managed the finances, learned to fix the car, worked in a defense plant, and wrote letters to their soldier husbands.

Rosie the Riveter helped assure that the Allies would have the war materials they needed. Nearly nineteen- million women held jobs during World War II. The Great Depression ended at the beginning of WWII.

Roosevelt was both a Jew-hater and a racist. He was in fact, eugenicist. He was against interracial marriage becoming legal. And he refused to do anything about the "KKK." One of FDR's Supreme Court appointees was Alabama Senator Hugo Black. Black was a member of the Ku Klux Klan, commonly shortened to the KKK. The KKK was a white supremacist terrorist and hate group whose primary targets were Black Americans and Jews. Roosevelt was indeed a racist. He refused to meet with Jessie Owens when Owens returned from the 1936 Olympic Games where he earned a Gold Medal after defeating

Hitlers Aryan athletes. Owens later quipped, "Hitler didn't stiff me, my own president did." He also hated Asians. His reprehensible internment of Japanese Americans during World War Two remains the worst action undertaken by an American president in the modern era.

Hugo Black

Jim Crow Laws mandated the segregation of public schools, public places, public transportation, segregation of restrooms, restaurants, and drinking fountains for whites and blacks. Named after a Black minstrel show character, the laws, which existed for about a hundred years, from the post-Civil War era until 1968, were meant to marginalize African Americans by denying them the right to vote, hold jobs, get an education or other opportunities. Those who attempted to defy Jim Crow laws often faced arrest, fines, jail sentences, violence, and death. Jim Crow laws were re-enacted in the late 19th and early 20th centuries by white Democratic-dominated state legislatures to disenfranchise and remove political and economic gains made by black people.

Roosevelt initially followed a continuation of the "gentleman's agreement" within the Democratic party that Northern Democrats would not interfere in race issues on the behalf of Black Americans.

Redlining followed the Great Depression. During Roosevelt's New Deal, the Federal Housing Administration provided white people with loan guarantees to banks, and it did not make loans available to blacks. Banks would often lend in lower-income white neighborhoods but not in middle-income or even upper-income black neighborhoods. The banking practice of classifying certain neighborhoods as not worthy of investment due to the racial makeup of their residents enabled whites to pull far ahead in equity gains.

Dr. Victor Frankl

And then came the Holocaust! Between 1941 and 1945, Nazi Germany and its collaborators systematically murdered some six million Jews, around two-thirds of Europe's Jewish population. Shortly after surviving the Holocaust, the Jewish neurologist, **Dr. Viktor Frankl** authored a book entitled *Man's Search for Meaning,* in which he described the horror of his imprisonment at Auschwitz. Prior to being sent to Auschwitz, Frankl served as head of the department of neurology at the Rothschild Hospital in Vienna. The Nazis closed Rothschild Hospital. His wife Tilly died in the Bergen Belsen concentration camp. Frankl, his parents, and his brother were sent to Theresienstadt concentration camp, where his father died of starvation. Frankl, his mother, and brother were then sent to Auschwitz concentration camp. Soon after their arrival, his mother and brother were taken to the gas chamber. Stripped of all material possessions, draped in rags, his body turned to skin and bones, Frankl, on his hands and knees, looked up into the staring eyes of the prison guard who was pulling Frankl's wedding ring from his scrawny finger. Soon he would have nothing but his remembrance of the past. From that moment of profound desperation came Dr. Frankl's thought which was equally profound. Everything could be taken from man, his possessions, his family, his health, and his freedom. What could not be taken was *man's greatest freedom.*

"Man's greatest freedom is that he gets to choose his attitude with any given set of circumstances!"

Dr. Frankl's thought is possibly the most profound philosophical lesson that I have ever learned. It has influenced my life in a very positive way.

George McGovern

Roosevelt, in fact, did many things to hinder the saving of Jews. **George Stanley McGovern** was an American historian and South Dakota politician who was a US representative and three-term US senator, and the Democratic Party presidential nominee in the 1972 presidential election. George McGovern, in a 2004 interview about the missions he flew near Auschwitz as a young bomber pilot, said:

> *Franklin Roosevelt was a great man, and he was my political hero. But I think he made two great mistakes: the internment of Japanese Americans, and the decision not to go after Auschwitz.... God forgive us.... There was a pretty good chance we could have blasted those rail lines off the face of the earth [and] interrupted the flow of people to those death chambers, and we had a pretty good chance of knocking out those gas ovens.*

Roosevelt's response to the Holocaust is no more defensible than his internment of Japanese Americans or his troubling record on the rights of Black Americans. Mentioning these "Historical Facts" does not endanger the legacy of the New Deal or diminish FDR's accomplishments in bringing America out of the Depression or his leadership in World War II. It merely acknowledges his flaws as well.

At the time, America needed a strong president and Roosevelt was the man.

In addition to being strong, FDR was incredibly superstitious! He would never light more than three cigarettes off the same match, declined to sit at table set for thirteen, and would not start a trip on a Friday. Ironically, FDR's funeral took his body back home on a train from Georgia commenced on Friday the 13th.

Roosevelt was a chain-smoker throughout his entire adult life, he had declining physical health since his late fifties.

With his failing health Roosevelt asked Eleanor to come home and live with him, she refused.

FDR died at sixty-three on April 12, 1945, with his great love, Lucy at his side.

CHAPTER FIVE

And then there was me

F our Score and five years ago, about halfway through Roosevelt's time as the Commander in Chief of the United States, I came to Earth on Tuesday, May 24, 1938, at 3:45 p.m. at Mary's Help Hospital in San Francisco, California. My mom told me I came down the chute feet first and had my umbilical cord wrapped around my neck. If the doctor, Ray Harris had not unwrapped it quickly, this would have been a very short book. Well, feet-first is pretty much the way I've traveled through life.

In April of 1938, one month before me, Superman came to Earth. Superman was faster than a speeding bullet. Superman could leap tall buildings in a single bound. Superman could see through walls, and Superman could fly. I had a defective seeing right eye and never even learned to crawl! I would lie on my backside and push with my feet to get around. That's why the back of my head has a flat spot. I also was slow learning to walk. Great start to a wonderful life. Superman had only Kryptonite, a green, crystalline material originating from Superman's home world of Krypton that emits a unique radiation that weakens Kryptonians. I, on the other hand, found a world filled to the brim with obstacles to overcome.

Time Magazine made Adolf Hitler the "Man of the Year" in 1938 and they didn't so much as mention the birth of LeRoy Bain.

Considering World War II began in 1939, I entered this world at an interesting time. The only recollection I have of Franklin D. Roosevelt was often seeing him in Newsreels during double-feature old west cowboy movies at the Granada theater. Two movies, a newsreel, and a cartoon, all for a hard-earned fifteen cents.

Every school day morning, a busload of Japanese children was brought to our school from detention centers where they were kept. Living in a coastal city, air raid warnings were a frequent occurrence in San Francisco. At school, we had air-raid drills. We were trained to crawl under our desk. I'm sure that would have saved me from an exploding bomb.

At home in the evening, all residents would turn out the lights, pull down the window blinds and sit in the dark listening to the radio. We listened to The Amos and Andy Show, two white guys mimicking black people. Jack Armstrong the All-American Boy; a white boy, I am sure. The violin-playing comedian, Jack Benny. Benny portrayed himself as a miser who played his violin badly and claimed perpetually to be thirty-nine years of age. The Lone Ranger, a masked cowboy and Tonto his Indian compadre. Listening to the radio with its canned laugher and many sound effects was more fun than you might imagine. There were no "radio dinners," and no microwave in which you could cook them. Television and computers were a few years off. We had an "ice box." We would put the milk that had a layer of cream at the top, and came in a glass bottle, either in the ice box or on the window seal, whichever was colder. We would listen to three or four radio programs a night. My parents blamed the radio for me not doing my homework.

As part of the war effort, my brother, sister, and I collected tinfoil. We spent hours walking the streets, searching for and picking up cigarette packages and gum wrappers. We would separate the tinfoil from the paper backing and then roll it into a tin-foil ball to be sold as junk metal. From our neighbors, we collected old newspapers which we tied into bundles. Nothing was thrown out; it was collected and sold to the junk man. The junk man with his horse-drawn wagon came down the street every Saturday.

As children we would sing this little song:

"Whistle while you work, Hitler is a jerk.
Mussolini is a weeny, and the Japs are worse!"

During the Second World War, "KILROY WAS HERE," became a popular cultural expression. The American GI put this graffiti on walls and fences all over Europe. I'm sure I was not the only kid named LeRoy who acquired the nickname KILROY.

When the war was over, on VJ Day, (Victory over Japan Day), 1945, the streetcars in San Francisco were packed with servicemen returning home. We had great fun asking for and collecting souvenirs. We got a lot of Japanese money. One sailor showed me his pocket full of what he said were Japanese soldiers' ears. He said he cut them off himself.

In my lifetime there have been fifteen presidents of the United States, seven Republicans and eight Democrats. I have liked and voted for some of each. As previously stated, I don't vote for a candidate based on which political party they belong. I believe in a two-party system that has kept America balanced and that balance is very important for a nation to survive the different philosophies of its people. It's a "teeter totter" with the Democrat Party on the left side and the Republican Party on the right side. It's zero-sum equation: when one side goes up, the opposite side goes down. The net change in these situations is zero since it is neither destroyed nor created, just redistributed. The "riders" are the American voters that move in the direction of the ideology of the party in power. Each party usually goes too far in one direction for the liking of the American people, and they move to the opposite side causing the emotional seesaw to teeter. The fulcrum on which the seesaw tetters is also a counterbalance. The counterbalance is the "American Constitution!" America is not just great because of all the hard-working people. While hard work is important to American success, the reason America is great is the plan. The American plan is the American Constitution. The Constitution is our set of rules by which we have lived for over 250 years. The two sides of the teeter totter do a lot of teetering; the fulcrum is stable and causes a balance of power. I make my voting decision based on what I believe our country needs at the time.

Sometimes we need the kind-hearted "Mother Teresa," and sometimes we need hard-nosed "Dirty Harry!" Sometimes we end up with, a president who is a "Serial Womanizer," and sometimes we end up with "Mr. Magoo!"

I believe who the current president is, to a great degree, dictates who the next president will be. An example of the pendulum swinging from one party to the other because of corruption came in 1968 when **Richard Nixon** named **Spiro Agnew** as his vice-president. Agnew took kickbacks when he was governor of Maryland which continued into his vice presidency. After months of maintaining his innocence, Agnew pleaded no contest to a single charge of tax evasion and resigned from office. In 1974 Nixon resigned rather than be impeached for covering up illegal activities of party members in the Watergate affair. Nixon was also known as "Tricky Dick." The American voters perceived the Nixon administration as dishonest and corrupt and wanted their next choice to be a nice, honest guy.

Along came **Jimmy Carter** with a Bible tucked under his arm. While the peanut farmer was a very nice guy, President Carter was considered by voters to be a weak "do-nothing" president. After four years of Carter, the voters wanted a strong positive leader and along came **Ronald Reagan**. Looking back allows us to see how cause and effect influences our lives.

It is my belief that,

> "When a country has hard times such as the Great Depression, its people become strong, a country with strong people build prosperous times, prosperous times cause weak people and weak people bring about hard times."
> Around and around, up and down, we go.
> It's Circular Logic!

Living my life in America with fifteen different presidents with fifteen different governing philosophies has caused me to experience and endure the good, the bad and the ugly which came with the many different leaders. For example, you will probably find it interesting how many presidents had extramarital affairs while in the White House. In this book I will attempt to shine a light on each of our last fifteen presidents and explain how it may affect the lifestyle which you enjoy because of our AMERICAN FREEDOM!

Quoting words from Lee Greenwood's song,

> *"I'm proud to be an American where at least I know I'm FREE! and I won't forget the men who died and gave that right to me.*

Roy and Lee

How are your mathematical skills?

Start by choosing a number from one to nine; subtract five. If your answer is negative, that's OK. Next multiply by three. Then multiply your number by itself. If your answer is made up of more than one digit, add the numbers together until you have just one digit. (Example if your number is 139. Add the one to three to nine that equals thirteen. You now have two digits so add the one to the three that equals four.) Now if your number is less than five, add five; if it is over five subtract four. Multiply by two and subtract three. Now locate the corresponding letter in the alphabet (1=a, 2=b, 3=c and so on.) Pick a state that begins with that letter. Next think of the name of a mammal that begins with the second letter of the state you have chosen. What is the color of the mammal?

Keep your answer in mind, I will refer to it later!

Franklin D. Roosevelt remains the only president to serve more than two terms. (The 22nd Amendment passed in 1951 set term limits as the president to two four-year terms.)

When FDR ran for his fourth term as president, he was unhappy with his vice president, Henry Wallace. FDR dropped Wallace and selected Truman as his vice president for his fourth term.

Harry S Truman

When Truman entered the room at FDR's funeral no one stood up. After twelve years of Roosevelt's commanding presence, it was hard for people to accept this spectacled haberdasher as chief executive. "The Haberdasher" was one of Truman's nicknames.

After the funeral, President Harry Truman arrived at the White House, where he was greeted by FDR's widow, Eleanor.

Truman asked Eleanor,

> "Is there anything we can do for you?"

And Eleanor replied,

> "For me? You're the one in trouble now!"

Harry and Eleanor

Harry S Truman

Harry S Truman became the thirty-third president of the United States, serving from 1945 to 1953.

Truman was born in Lamar, Missouri, on May 8, 1884, the oldest child of John Anderson Truman and Martha Ellen Young Truman. Harry was named "Harry" for his maternal uncle, Harrison "Harry" Young. His middle initial, "S," honors his grandfathers, Anderson **S**hipp Truman and **S**olomon Young. There is no period "." after the "S" in Truman's name. Harry wore thick glasses starting very young. Harry was not allowed to play outside with the other kids. Harry's mother insisted he rise at 5:00 a.m. every morning to practice the piano, which he studied more than twice a week until he was fifteen. He became quite good and enjoyed entertaining friends at church.

Harry

Harry was a poor country boy. His parents were farmers who had difficulty making a living. When Harry was six, his parents moved to Independence, Missouri.

In Independence, Harry attended the Presbyterian Church Sunday School. It was at this school he met Bess Wallace, his future wife at six years old. He did not attend a public school until he was eight. At age ten, Harry contracted diphtheria and spent almost a year with his arms, legs and throat paralyzed. He eventually recovered but became even more frail and shy.

Bess

After graduating from Independence High School in 1901, Harry enrolled in Spalding's Commercial College, a Kansas City business school. He studied bookkeeping, shorthand, and typing but dropped out after part of one year when he was requested to return home to help on the family farm. Through these trying times he enjoyed a relationship with his high school sweetheart Bess.

In 1903, when Bess was 18, her father rose very early one morning, climbed into the family bathtub, and shot himself in the head. He left no note, it was believed his suicide was the result of mounting debts and a depression heightened by heavy drinking.

Harry worked a variety of odd jobs as a young man, including a timekeeper for the Santa Fa Railroad. During this time, he would sleep in hobo camps. Because of his poverty, his proposal to Bess Wallace was rejected, which was a turning point in his life, motivating him to make more money. He applied to West Point but was rejected because of his poor eyesight. Harry joined the National Guard in 1905.

In 1911, when he was twenty-seven, Harry wrote to Bess: "I think one man is just as good as another so long as he's honest and decent and not a 'n-word' or a Chinaman. Uncle Will says that the Lord made a white man from dust, a 'n-word' from mud, then he threw up what was left, and it came down a Chinaman." "Uncle Will does hate Chinese and Japs," Harry continued. "So, do I. It is race prejudice, I guess. But I am strongly of the opinion N-words ought to be in Africa, yellow men in Asia and white men in Europe and America."

The Great War, later known as **World War One (WWI)**, started in 1914 and was one of the deadliest conflicts in history. An estimated nine million were killed in combat, while over five million civilians died from bombardment, hunger, or disease. When the war started, the Great Powers were divided into two opposing alliances, the first *consisting of France, Russia, and Britain,* and the opposition made up of *Germany, Austria, Hungary, and Italy.* On January 19, 1917, German high command sent a message to Mexico asking Mexico to join WWI by attacking the USA. Mexico alerted Washington to Berlin's plan, which brought the previously neutral United States into the war. In late 1917, Truman's National Guard unit was called up for basic training. Just before he left, Truman got a message from Bess saying she decided to marry him after all. Truman responded, "I don't think it would be right for me to ask you to tie yourself to a prospective cripple, or a sentiment." In March of 1918, Truman was promoted to captain in field artillery and by August was fighting on the front lines. Through September and October, he fought in the bloody Meuse-Argonne offensive.

The Great War Artillery

The **Meuse-Argonne Offensive** was the largest operation of the American Expeditionary Forces (AEF) in WWI, with over a million American soldiers participating. **Truman was a war hero who saw action in battle.**

The only future president to see action in the great war, Truman gained his first experience leading men. Truman was the first president in thirty-six years since, Theodore "Teddy" Roosevelt, to be in the United States military. He developed a friendship with a soldier by the name of **Jim Prendergast**. A connection that would change his life.

Facing revolution at home and an army on the verge of mutiny, Kaiser Wilhelm abdicated on November 9, 1918 and the new German government signed the Armistice bringing the fighting to a close.

Bess Truman

During this period, Truman wrote letters to Bess often during their long courtship, and his letters were filled with dreams for their future. Harry returned to Missouri in May of 1919. One month later, he and Bess were married on June 28th.

Not long after, the Trumans worked together in a clothing store they opened in Kansas City, but the Trumans failed in business and the young couple moved in with her wealthy grandparents and her mother. Harry was embarrassed by his business failure and was committed to paying back every debt he owed to those who had given him credit. He spent most of his life paying the debt. Harry and Bess had one daughter, Margaret. In 1922 Harry sat in his mother-in-law's house in a small town in Missouri. He was depressed contemplating his life and all his failures. He was nearly forty and behind him lay a string of failed businesses and unfulfilling odd jobs. He was deeply in debt, close to bankrupt, and looked down upon by his wife's elitist family.

Thomas Joseph Pendergast (who was the uncle of Truman's WWI buddy, Jim Pendergast) was an American political boss who controlled Kansas City and Jacksonville County, MO from 1925 to 1939. Pendergast only briefly held elected office, as an alderman. As chairman of the Jackson County Democrat Party, he used his large network of family and friends to help the election of politicians. In some cases, there was *voter fraud*, and he handed out large government contracts to friends without competitive bids. The Pendergast organization helped to launch the political career of future United States President Harry S Truman, which caused Truman's early enemies to dub him "The Senator from Pendergast."

Truman's honesty became questionable due to the democratic machine's corruption, and yet, people overlooked his dishonesty and made him a judge of Jackson County, Missouri. Harry did his bosses biding by awarding fat contracts to Pendergast's allies.

In 1934, Pendergast was persuaded to support Truman, whom he considered somewhat of a lightweight, for the Democratic nomination for a US Senate seat. Pendergast asked Truman how he would like to be a senator and just like that he was on his way to congress.

While very smart with an IQ of 127, Truman is the only president since William McKinley (elected in 1896) who did not earn a college degree. While Truman was in the U.S. Senate, his analysis of defense contracts saved the government billions of dollars. Truman loved being a senator, except FDR had bigger plans for him and convinced Harry to become his vice-presidential candidate in 1944. Truman had a potty mouth. When he was first told about FDR's request to be his vice-presidential running mate, Truman said, "Tell him to go to hell."

Truman went from small town loser to eventually become the leader of the free world.

Senator Truman wrote a letter to his daughter, Margaret, describing waiters at the White House as "an army of coons." In a letter to Bess in 1939 he referred to "n-word picnic day." In 1941, in a letter to Margaret, he wrote of the Civil War, "I feel as your old country grandmother has expressed it, what a pity a white man like Lee had to surrender to old Grant."

Roosevelt kept Truman in the dark about war matters.

During his first few weeks as vice president, Harry scarcely saw FDR, and received no briefing on the development of the atomic bomb or the unfolding difficulties with Soviet Russia.

The Manhattan Project

The Manhattan Project was a research and development undertaking during World War II that produced the first nuclear weapons. It had been kept secret from the world until after Roosevelt's death.

The project was under the direction of Major General Leslie Groves of the US Army Corps of Engineers. Nuclear physicist Robert Oppenheimer was the director of the Los Alamos Laboratory that designed the actual bombs.

The big secret was kept from everyone except the Soviet Union. **Julius** and **Ethel Rosenberg** were American citizens who were convicted of spying on behalf of the Soviet Union. The couple were convicted of providing top-secret information about radar, sonar, jet propulsion engines and valuable nuclear weapon designs. Convicted of espionage in 1951, they were executed by the federal government of the United States in 1953 at Sing-Sing Prison in Ossining, New York, becoming the first American civilians to be executed for such charges and the first to receive that penalty during peacetime.

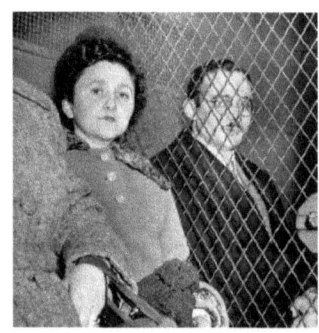

Julius and Ethel Rosenberg

After the fall of the Soviet Union, much information concerning them was declassified, including a trove of decoded Soviet cables, which detailed Julius's role as a courier and recruiter for the Soviets. Ethel's role was as an accessory who helped recruit her brother David into the spy ring and did clerical tasks such as typing up documents that Julius then passed to the Soviets. Suddenly these and a host of other wartime problems became Truman's to solve when, on April 12, 1945, FDR died, and he became president.

Truman told reporters,

> "I felt like the moon, the stars, and all the planets had fallen on me."

Known as the plain-speaking man from Missouri, Truman began his presidency with great energy. He, along with Winston Churchill and Joseph Stalin helped negotiate Germany's unconditional surrender in May 1945, which ended World War II in Europe. This happened after Truman was in office for just one month and the agreement was accomplished by Roosevelt prior to his death.

Little Boy

Atomic bomb Hiroshima

The war with Japan was still in progress when Truman authorized the dropping of the atomic bomb. On August 6, 1945, the American bomber "*Enola Gay*" dropped the five-ton bomb, **Little Boy** on the Japanese city of Hiroshima. A blast equivalent to the power of fifteen thousand tons of TNT which reduced four square miles of the city to ruins and immediately killed eighty thousand people. Tens of thousands more died in the following weeks from wounds and radiation poisoning. When the Japanese didn't surrender after the first bomb destroyed Hiroshima, President Truman three days later, ordered the second atomic bomb called, **Fat Man** be dropped on Nagasaki, killing nearly forty thousand more people. The two bombings killed more than 120,000 men, women, and children.

Atomic bomb Nagasaki

Fat Man

A few days later, Japan announced its surrender. It became official on September 2, 1945.

Truman received credit for ending World War II.

After the war in 1947, Jackie Robinson broke the baseball color line when he started at first base for the Brooklyn Dodgers on April 15, 1947. When the Dodgers signed Robinson, it heralded the end of racial segregation in professional baseball that had relegated black players to the Negro leagues since the 1880s. Robinson was inducted into the Baseball Hall of Fame in 1962.

Jackie Robinson

Truman marshaled his New Deal coalition during the 1948 election and won a surprise victory that secured his own presidential term. A young Democrat, **Ronald Reagan** campaigned for Truman in 1948. When he took the oath of office for his second term, Harry Truman had an ambitious agenda. He hoped to enact national health insurance, public housing, civil rights legislation, and federal aid to education. Harry Truman was sworn in for his second term in January 1949; his inauguration was the first to be nationally televised.

Truman's custom Limo

Stalin feared that Germany would recover from WWII, and they would be back at war with Russia. He demanded that Russia have a postwar buffer zone settling for a wall separating East from West Berlin. Churchill called the wall "The Iron Curtain." In 1948, when Russia blockaded the western sectors of Berlin, Truman created a massive airlift to supply Berliners until the Russians backed down.

Meanwhile, Truman was negotiating a military alliance to protect Western nations. Truman, in 1949, played a key role in establishing the **North Atlantic Treaty Organization, (NATO).**

The Plot to Assassinate President Truman!

In 1948 the White House was physically unsound and needed to be remodeled, so the first family moved to the Blair House. Blair House, also known as The President's Guest House. At 2:20 p.m. on November 1, 1950, Griselio Torresola approached the Pennsylvania Avenue entrance from the west. Oscar Collazo came from the east. White House police guarded the entrance. Terrorist Torresola was shot in the head and died. His partner, Collazo survived and was sentenced to death. One of the three police officers who were wounded died. The Secret Service's day room at Blair House is now named the Leslie W. Coffelt Memorial Room in honor of the officer who died in the attempt. Truman was upstairs taking a nap. He came to the window when he heard the noise but remained safe.

Truman wrote about FBI director **J. Edgar Hoover** during his presidency: "We want no Gestapo or secret police. The FBI is trending in that direction. They are dabbling in sex-life scandals and plain blackmail. Hoover would give his right eye to take over, and all congressmen and senators are afraid of him. The FBI operates secretly with little or no accountability to anyone!"

Truman and Hoover

On June 25, 1950, **The Korean Conflict** started. The conflict was a civil war fought between North and South Korea. China and the Soviet Union supported North Korea to expand communism. The United States joined the war and supported South Korea to contain communism and to expand Freedom. Forty thousand Americans died in action in Korea, and more than one hundred thousand were wounded. The fighting ended with an armistice on July 27, 1953, when the United States and the Soviet Union divided Korea along the thirty-eight parallel into two zones of occupation.

As the Korean War dragged on, the now Senator Joseph McCarthy made people paranoid that a communist spy was hiding in their closet. Poor Harry was portrayed as weak on communism and lacked ambition to address security matters. Truman had helped transform America into a world superpower, and historians now rank Truman among the nation's best presidents.

The sign "The Buck Stops Here" that was on President Truman's desk in his White House office was made in the Federal Reformatory at El Reno, Oklahoma. Fred A. Canfil, then United States marshal for the Western District of Missouri and a friend of Mr. Truman, saw a similar sign while visiting the reformatory and asked the Warden if a sign like it could be made for President Truman. The sign was made and mailed to the President on October 2, 1945.

The same man who admitted to harboring "race prejudice" *also* did more for civil rights than any previous president. He desegregated the armed forces. He named the first blacks to the federal bench, pushing Congress to pass an anti-lynching law, strengthening the Justice Department's civil rights division, and issuing an executive order instituting fair employment practice in the federal government.

FDR, as is well known, resisted pleas that he help rescue Europe's Jews from the Holocaust. On civil rights, FDR pointedly refused to desegregate the military, declined to confront southern senators on anti-lynching legislation, and pressured black leaders to call off planned protest marches during World War II.

For all his sympathetic words to Jews and blacks, FDR failed to deliver. For all his hostile words, Truman delivered. As the old saying goes, **Actions speak louder than words.** It was never truer when it came to Harry Truman.

Towards the end of Truman's term in office the United States Steel Workers of America and other major steel mine owners went out on strike. Truman seized the steel mills in the name of the government. The steel companies filed a suit referred to as the *Steel Seizure Case* that went to the United States Supreme Court. The Supreme Court ruled in favor of the steel companies. Truman lost his Supreme Court battle, and his reputation was vastly tarnished.

Housing and consumer good shortages caused tremendous public stress over inflation which peaked at 6 percent in a single month.

During his two terms in office, Truman appointed four members of the Supreme Court of the United States:

Chief Justice Fred M. Vinson, Associate Justice Harold Burton, Associate Justice Tom C. Clark, and Associate Justice Sherman Minton. When Supreme Court Associate Justice Owen J. Roberts retired in 1945, Truman decided to appoint a Republican as a bipartisan gesture.

When Truman left the presidency in January 1953, he was one of the most unpopular politicians in the United States. The Korean War and accusations of corruption in his administration contributed to the President's poor standing with the public. Truman was eligible to run again because the newly passed 22nd Amendment did not apply to the incumbent president at that time, but with weak polls, Truman chose not to run again in 1953.

A few of Truman's famous quotes were:

"The Buck Stops Here!"

"It is amazing what you can accomplish if you do not care who gets the credit."

"If you can't stand the heat, get out of the kitchen!"

After his presidency, Truman and his wife Bess returned to Independence, Missouri, where popular lore suggests he led a relatively pauper-like existence. For a short time after leaving Washington, Truman's income was principally from a small pension of $1,350 a year (roughly $13,800, adjusted for inflation)—from his stint in the army, not as commander-in-chief. And he famously turned down high-paying corporate jobs, believing that cashing in on his name was below the office of the presidency. But he signed the rights to his memoir for six hundred thousand dollars in the mid-1950s, more than six million dollars in today's dollars, which was reportedly paid out over several years.

Truman retired to Independence; at the age of eighty-eight, he died December 26, 1972, of old age rather than any illness.

CHAPTER SEVEN

Dwight D. Eisenhower

D wight was born on October 14, 1890, in Denison, Texas. Both of Dwight's parents were of German descent and were Mennonites. Interesting considering Eisenhower spent WWII fighting against Germany.

Dwight

The Eisenhower's were a poor family and Dwight was often made fun of for wearing ragged clothing and his mother's old shoes. Dwight was the third of seven sons. The family relocated to Kansas, where Dwight's older brother was nicknamed "Big Ike," in school and he became tagged as "Little Ike." Little Ike played baseball and football at Abilene High School. After Dwight graduated from high school in 1909, he went to work with his father at the Belle Springs Creamery while also moonlighting as a fireman. He joined the army on "Flag Day," June 14, 1911. He then decided to go to the United States Military Academy at **West Point**, New York. The nickname "Ike" stayed with him at West Point, where the "Little" for a just under six-foot-tall soldier was inappropriate. At West Point, he was a star football player until his knees gave out and forced him to leave the sport.

Ike's abysmal academic performance at West Point may not have been the sole reason he graduated 61st in a class of 164. He was a notorious prankster! For silly instance, his commanding officer told him to appear in full dress coat. Well, he promptly showed up in his dress coat, and that was it! No shoes or socks, no shirt, and no pants. His commanding officer didn't laugh, he commented, "You're dressed okay for a flasher, not for a soldier!"

Eisenhower constantly broke the rules and regulations at West Point. The list of his demerits runs nearly ten pages. Biographer Carlo D'Este writes that Eisenhower "seemed to relish every opportunity to outwit an instructor or upperclassman." Eisenhower's willful disregard for the rules pertaining to dancing, for example, brought him to the attention of the commandant. Eisenhower ignored an order not to, in his words, "whirl" a professor's daughter during a dance. His willfulness led the commandant to demote him, confine him to barracks and order him to walk twenty-two laps.

Eisenhower devoted his energies to football, a sport he had played in high school. Two weeks after competing against the legendary, Olympic gold medalist Jim Thorpe, Eisenhower suffered a major knee injury. That injury and others almost led an Army doctor to recommend that the future general be allowed to graduate but not receive a commission.

West Point officials eventually settled on a commission in the infantry. Eisenhower was deployed to the Mexican border, one of the least sought-after deployments in that era.

Ultimately, the best parts of college for Eisenhower were the lessons he learned about leadership and the friends he made among his classmates. Those classmates, collectively known as the "class the stars fell on," eventually rose high in the ranks and formed a cadre of allies Eisenhower would call upon later.

Ike graduated and was commissioned on June 12, 1915, a Second Lieutenant. Ike was stationed in Texas, where he started dating **Mamie Geneva Doud**. Unlike Ike, Mamie came from a very wealthy family in Iowa. Ike was 24 years old; Mamie was 18 when they met. The couple married nine months later, on July 1, 1916. Ike was promoted to **First Lieutenant** on their wedding day.

Mamie Eisenhower

Ike and Mamie Eisenhower's first son, Doud Dwight, was born on September 24, 1917. Little "Ikey" was a happy child, but as Christmas 1920 approached, he fell ill with scarlet fever. The illness soon became meningitis, and the three-year-old died on the second day of January in 1921. The following year the couple had their only other child, John. (Interesting data: Life expectancy in 1900 was forty-seven years. One of the major reasons was the number of deaths of newborn and children before the discovery of antibiotics.) Eisenhower rose through the ranks and by 1920, after volunteering for the Tank Corps, he was promoted to major. In 1933 Ike served as chief military aide to General Douglas MacArthur in the Philippines. He thought MacArthur to be an *egomaniac* with little regard for anyone else. Notice the difference in their uniforms in this photo. MacArthur wore every medal he had received, Eisenhower wore none. Eisenhower had a lot of experience with egos. He dealt with General Bernard

MacArthur and Eisenhower

Gen. Patton with his pearl-handled revolvers

Montgomery and General George S. Patton, but MacArthur had the biggest ego of them all. In 1942 Eisenhower was promoted to acting major general. Just months later, he became commander-in-chief of the Allied Forces and led

Operation Torch, the Allied invasion of North Africa. On February 11, 1943, Eisenhower became an acting four-star General.

The general and his aide

A good-looking soldier, Kay Summersby was Ike's driver and aide during World War II. The Eisenhower and Summersby romance are among the most debated topics by Eisenhower biographers. The great love affair between Kay and the general was well known; however, it was believed they had not actually had sexual intercourse. Their physical relationship was limited, both by the demands of the war and by Eisenhower's rumored inability to perform due to erectile dysfunction. But apparently the relationship was emotionally significant.

On June 11, 1942, although Eisenhower had never seen combat during his twenty-seven years as an army officer, his knowledge of military strategy and talent for organization were such that Army Chief of Staff General George C. Marshall chose him over nearly four hundred senior officers to lead US forces in the war against Germany. On August 30, 1943, Ike was appointed to both brigadier general and major general on the same date. Unlike his previous acting promotions, both were permanent ranks. After proving himself on the battlefields of North Africa and Italy in 1942 and 1943, Eisenhower arrived at US headquarters in London and took command.

Eisenhower designed Operation Overlord, *the largest combined sea, air, and land military operation in history*. Overlord was successfully launched against Nazi-occupied Europe which included the Normandy invasion on June 6, 1944. The codename for the invasion, which is remembered, and honored today was "D-Day."

On May 7, 1945, Germany surrendered.

By that time, Eisenhower was a **Five-Star General**.

After the war, Eisenhower replaced Marshall as army chief of staff from 1948 to 1950.

After a brief respite from the military as the president of Columbia University, Eisenhower was called back to active duty. President Harry S Truman appointed him the Supreme Commander of **NATO**. He served in this position until 1952.

Eisenhower earned a reputation as a superb negotiator. His American and British subordinates often were as ready to fight themselves as they were to fight the Germans. He struggled to make them work together effectively against the Third Reich. His brilliant leadership ability was believed to be "White House" worthy. He relinquished his NATO command to run for president on the Republican ticket.

During his presidential campaign, Eisenhower's television ads included twenty-second spots titled "Eisenhower Answers the Nation." First, the camera would go to the concerned party who would ask a question followed by the camera moving to Eisenhower for his response. This was much more appreciated by the public than the thirty-minute ads produced by opponent Adlai E. Stevenson. Eisenhower was not a fan of the ads; he thought, to think that an old soldier has come to this. However, they were magnificently successful.

Adlai Stevenson

In November 1952, "Ike" won a resounding victory in the presidential elections with Richard Nixon as his vice president.

General Dwight David Eisenhower attacked Harry Truman's record and won easily in 1952 to become the thirty-fourth President of the United States, a Republican.

Dwight D. Eisenhower

Ike's prestige as commanding general of the victorious forces in Europe during World War II helped obtain a truce in Korea.

Adlai Stevenson was Eisenhower's opponent both in 1952 and again in 1956. In 1948, Stevenson was elected governor of Illinois, defeating incumbent governor Dwight H. Green in an upset. As governor, he reformed the state police, cracked down on illegal gambling, improved the state highways, and attempted to cleanse the state government of corruption. However, his efforts at constitutional reform and the crime bills failed to pass the state legislature.

In the 1952 and 1956 presidential elections, Stevenson was chosen as the Democratic nominee for president but was defeated in a landslide by Republican Eisenhower both times.

Eisenhower and Nixon take oath for their second term

Ike was a popular president and oversaw a period of great economic growth in the United States. He successfully navigated the country through increasing Cold War tensions on the world stage.

The rallying call for Eisenhowers campaign

Eisenhower thought government should be as modest as possible. Despite being a Republican president, many historians have noted that he is far more popular among Democrats and left-leaning Americans than conservatives.

At the time I was keenly aware of national politics. In 1956, I graduated high school, and the draft was on. Rather than being drafted, I decided to join and serve. My first choice was the navy, but when I met with the navy recruiter he asked, "Can you swim?" I answered, "Don't you have any boats?"

The Korean War was over in 1953 and the war in Vietnam had not started when I joined the Utah National Guard. The first six months were spent on active duty in the United States Army where I took my basic training at Fort Ord, California. I served in the Army National Guard for six "peace-time" years.

At one point, our unit was going to be activated and we were going to be sent to Laos. We had our duffel bags packed, our many shots, kissed our families goodbye and were ready to go. I must admit, going to war did not sound like a good future. The reason for the engagement was North Vietnam supported the Pathet Lao to fight against the Kingdom of Laos in 1958. Control over Laos allowed for the eventual construction of the Ho Chi Minh Trail that would serve as the main supply route for the National Liberation Front, the Vietcong, and North Vietnamese Army activities in the Republic of Vietnam. The engagement was cancelled, and I was happy to stay home. Being at home in the Guard gave me the opportunity to serve my country while at the same time further my career.

Fidel Castro

When I was twenty-one in 1959, still a member of the National Guard, a young, charismatic Cuban nationalist named **Fidel Castro** with his friend **Ernesto "Ché" Guevara** led a guerrilla army against the forces of the Dictator General Fulgencio Batista on the island of Cuba. US backed Batista was forced to flee the country. Castro took control of the Cuban Government's thirty-thousand-man army and declared himself Prime Minister. With Castro as the prime minister, adopting a Marxist–Leninist model of development, Castro converted Cuba into a one-party, socialist state.

Ché

Cuba is located where the northern Caribbean Sea, Gulf of Mexico, and Atlantic Ocean meet. Cuba is just ninety miles off the US coast of Key West, Florida. Havana is the largest city and capital of Cuba. For nearly fifty years, Cuba had been America's playground and agricultural center. Many wealthy Americans lived in Cuba and had established thriving businesses there. In fact, a significant portion of Cuba's sugar plantations were owned by North Americans. With Castro's self-appointment to prime minister, that changed.

Castro and Khrushchev

The American-Cuban relationship deteriorated further when Castro established diplomatic relations with our Cold War rival, the Soviet Union. Castro and Soviet Premier Nikita Khrushchev signed a series of pacts that resulted in large deliveries of economic and military aid to Cuba in 1960. Within a year, Castro proclaimed himself a communist, formally allied his country with the Soviet Union, and seized remaining American and foreign-owned assets.

With Eisenhower's approval, the CIA was to conduct a covert operation to rid the island of Castro. The CIA formulated a plan to recruit Cuban exiles living in the Miami area. It would train and equip the exiles to infiltrate Cuba and start a revolution to ignite an uprising across the island and overthrow this self-appointed leader. The CIA did not finish this project while Eisenhower was in office, and it was dropped in the lap of his successor, John F. Kennedy. Kennedy messed it up, which we will discuss later.

At the time, I believed that Eisenhower was too old and did a poor job with Cuba. I remember saying Eisenhower was like the big guy in school, and Castro was a little guy that kept kicking the big guy in the leg and the big guy did nothing. I thought the big, strong guy should have picked the little guy up by the neck, looked him in the eye, and said, "Look! You kick me one more time and I'll blow you and your island off the map, so stop being a problem for America!" I believed that Ike did nothing.

Even though the Supreme Court of the United States had ruled against segregation, some local officials refused to integrate the schools. Eisenhower signed the Civil Rights Act of 1957 and sent army troops to enforce federal court orders which integrated schools in Little Rock, Arkansas.

One of Eisenhower's largest and best programs was America's Interstate Highway System. On June 29, 1956, Eisenhower signed the Federal-Aid Highway Act of 1956. The bill created a forty-one-thousand-mile "National System of Interstate and Defense Highways" that would, according to Eisenhower, eliminate unsafe roads, inefficient routes, traffic jams, and all of the other things that got in the way of "speedy, safe transcontinental travel." On July 29, 1958, Eisenhower signed the National Aeronautics and Space Act of 1958, establishing the National Aeronautics and Space Administration (**NASA**).

The last two American states, Alaska (49) and Hawaii (50), were admitted to the Union during Eisenhower's presidency. He nominated five members for the Supreme Court of the United States including Chief Justice Earl Warren and Justices John Marshall Harlan, William Brennan, Charles Evans Whittaker, and Potter Stewart. All were confirmed by the Senate. The Court moved from being totally liberal to more conservative.

Presidents Franklin D. Roosevelt and Harry Truman originally called the Maryland presidential retreat, which opened in 1938, "Shangri-La" after the fictional Himalayan paradise. Eisenhower renamed it in 1953 in honor of his five-year- old grandson, "Camp David." Soviet leader Nikita Khrushchev, who was brought by Eisenhower to the retreat, thought it sounded like a place where "stray dogs were sent to die," but President John F. Kennedy and all subsequent chief executives have kept the name.

In the spring of 1954, the American Public Golf Association installed an outdoor putting green just steps away from the Oval Office. To the dismay of Eisenhower, who was an avid golfer, the squirrels who roamed the White House grounds continually dug up the putting green to bury their acorns and walnuts. "The next time you see one of those squirrels go near my putting green, take a gun, and shoot it!" he ordered his valet, Sergeant John Moaney. The Secret Service, however, wisely avoided the use of guns, and instead, groundskeepers trapped the squirrels and released them into Rock Creek Park.

Martin Luther King Jr. was born on January 15, 1929. His birth name was Michael King Jr. King was an American Baptist minister and activist who became the most visible spokesman and leader in the civil rights movement from 1955 until his assassination in 1968. His nonviolence and civil disobedience activity was inspired by his Christian beliefs and the nonviolent activism of Mahatma Gandhi. King was one of the leaders of the 1963 March on Washington, where he delivered his "I Have a Dream" speech on the steps of the Lincoln Memorial. J. Edgar Hoover considered King a radical and made him an object of the FBI's CO-INTEL-PRO (counterintelligence program) from 1963 forward. FBI agents investigated King for possible communist ties, spied on his personal life and secretly and illegally recorded him.

Martin Luther King Jr.

On October 14, 1964, King won the Nobel Peace Prize for combating racial inequality through nonviolent resistance. In 1968 King was planning a national occupation of Washington DC, to be called the Poor Peoples Campaign, when he was assassinated on April 4th in Memphis, Tennessee. King was posthumously awarded the Presidential Medal of Freedom in 1977 and the Congressional Gold Medal in 2003.

In 1961, following his presidency, Eisenhower retired to a farmhouse in Gettysburg with his wife, Mamie. This was the first home that he and his wife purchased due to the time served in the army.

Eisenhower was an avid card player. He and Mamie were so obsessed with bridge and canasta that they had friends flown in to ensure there was enough players.

He detested having his golf game interrupted and when it was, he became enraged with absolute fury. Unfortunately, his rage caused him to suffer a massive heart attack. Dr. Snyder, Ike's personal physician, was so distraught with the president's condition that he broke down in tears. When the press learned of his heart attack, a tumultuous Monday followed, and the stock market lost fourteen billion dollars.

Subsequently, he suffered many more heart attacks until his death in 1969.

Eisenhower understandably became accustomed to having the details of his life managed for him. So much that he had people to dress him, put his watch on, and pull up his trousers.

This presented a problem after his presidency and he was almost unable to do the simplest tasks, such as dialing a telephone, turning on the TV, paying for merchandise at a store, and paying a tollbooth on the highway.

Eisenhower died on March 28, 1969, at Walter Reed Army Hospital in Washington, DC, following a long period of suffering from a heart-related illness. In addition to a state funeral in the nation's capital, a military funeral was held in Eisenhower's beloved hometown of Abilene, Kansas.

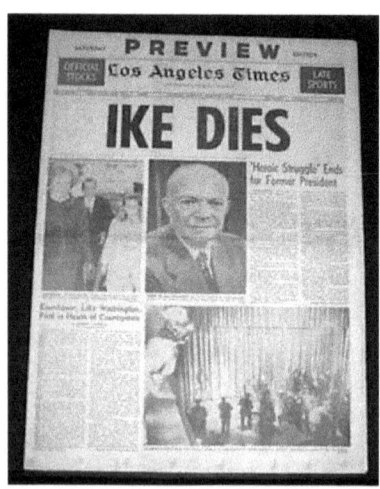

"Great General and leader.
He was a major reason we won WWII!

A few of Eisenhower's quotes:

"History does not long entrust the care of freedom to the weak or the timid."

"An intellectual is a man who takes more words than necessary to tell more than he knows."

"Motivation is the art of getting people to do what you want them to do because they want to do it."

"What counts is not necessarily the size of the dog in the fight – it's the size of the fight in the dog."

"Never waste a minute thinking about people you don't like."

"Extremes to the right and to the left of any political dispute are always wrong."

"A sense of humor is part of the art of leadership, of getting along with people, of getting things done."

"Leadership consists of nothing but taking responsibility for everything that goes wrong and giving your subordinates credit for everything that goes well."

CHAPTER EIGHT

John Fitzgerald Kennedy

John Fitzgerald Kennedy, a Democrat served as the thirty-fifth president of the United States from 1961 until November 22, 1963. Kennedy was one of America's smartest presidents with an estimated IQ of 158.

John Fitzgerald Kennedy

To understand John Fitzgerald Kennedy, I find it necessary to take a close look into the life and times of his father, Joseph Patrick Kennedy.

Jackie Kennedy

Before we examine Joseph Kennedy, I should mention, I turned twenty-one in May of 1961, and John Kennedy, often referred to by his initials JFK, was the first president for whom I voted. Unlike Eisenhower, in my opinion at the time, Kennedy seemed to have it all. He was young, very smart, well spoken, very good looking, and had a gorgeous first lady, **Jacqueline Bouvier Kennedy.** At the time I was proud to speak out in their favor.

It was my long-held belief that the Kennedy fortune came about through bootlegging and other illegal means. What an interesting story it would have been if I would have discovered it to be true. Over the years and especially after the assassination of JFK many have accused **Joseph Kennedy of being a friend of Al Capone and a bootlegger** during Prohibition. **However, my research reveals a much different tale.**

Richard Nixon, when he was running against JFK in 1960, hired a team of opposition researchers to investigate the Kennedy clan. They found all sorts of dirt on Joseph Kennedy, but none that suggested that he was a friend of Al Capone or a bootlegger.

Joseph Kennedy graduated from Harvard University in 1912. Two years later he married Rose Fitzgerald. Rose taught her nine children to be honest, compassionate, and to love. Joseph inspired a fierce competitive drive in his children. The Kennedy children were encouraged to read *the New York Times* at an early age, and small talk was not allowed at the dinner table.

Joseph was a bank president at age twenty-five and a millionaire at thirty. He got rich as a shipbuilder and later as a motion-picture tycoon. He became a brilliant stock-exchange manipulator when inside trading was legal in the 1920s.

Joseph, as chairman of the Securities and Exchange Commission (1934–35) under FDR, outlawed the very speculative practices that helped make him rich.

In the fall of 1933, when it became clear that Prohibition was going to be overturned, Kennedy used his already substantial wealth and political connections to land exclusive contracts to import high-end Scotch whiskey and gin from the United Kingdom. Those deals with top-shelf British distillers like Dewar's and Gordon's gin proved exceptionally lucrative. Kennedy sold his liquor franchise a decade later for over eight million, more than one hundred million in today's dollars. But that was mere pocket change to a man who had already amassed a fortune by the time he turned forty. He retired early in 1929, having acquired enough capital to establish a million-dollar trust fund for each of his children.

Joseph Kennedy was an invalid in Hyannis Port by a stroke for several years and died at age eighty-one. Rose Kennedy survived her husband by twenty-five years, dying at Hyannis Port on January 22, 1995, at age 104.

John Fitzgerald Kennedy was born in Brookline, Massachusetts on May 29, 1917. His paternal grandfather, P. J. Kennedy, served as a Massachusetts state legislator. Kennedy's maternal grandfather and namesake, John F. Fitzgerald, served as a US congressman and was elected to two terms as mayor of Boston. All four of his grandparents were children of Irish immigrants. Several years later, John's brother Robert told Look magazine that his father had left Boston because of signs that read: "No Irish Need Apply." Kennedy had an elder brother, Joseph Jr., and seven younger siblings: Rosemary, Kathleen, Eunice, Patricia, Robert, Jean, and Edward.

John

John enrolled at Harvard College in September 1936.

"To be a *'Harvard Man'* is an enviable distinction, and one that I sincerely hope I shall attain." He produced that year's annual "Freshman Smoker," considered by its readers, to be "an entertaining paper, which included personalities of the radio, and the sports world." Harvard has produced eight US presidents, more than any other school.

He found out he was not skilled enough for the football or golf teams. However, he was good enough to be on the Harvard varsity swimming team. Kennedy was also great at sailing and won the 1936 Nantucket Sound Star Championship. In July 1937, Kennedy sailed to France. He took his convertible with him and spent two and a half months driving through Europe with a friend.

When Kennedy was an upperclassman at Harvard, he began to take his studies more seriously and developed an interest in political philosophy. He made the dean's list in his junior year. In 1940, Kennedy completed his thesis, "Appeasement in Munich," about British negotiations during the Munich Agreement. The thesis eventually became a bestseller under the title *Why England Slept*. I have discovered that Joseph purchased thirty thousand copies of his son's book and kept them in the attic making John a best-selling author. In 1940, Kennedy graduated cum laude from Harvard with a Bachelor of Arts in government, concentrating on international affairs. That fall, he enrolled at the Stanford Graduate School of Business. In early 1941, he then traveled throughout South America.

Also, in 1940, due to his chronic lower back problems, he was medically disqualified to enter the army's Officer Candidate School. On September 24, 1941, Kennedy, with the help of then director of the Office of Naval Intelligence and the former naval attaché to Joseph Kennedy, Alan Kirk, joined the United States Naval Reserve. He was commissioned an Ensign on October 26, 1941, and joined the staff of the Office of Naval Intelligence in Washington, D.C.

After serving in a few safe staff jobs in the US, he went out of his way to get in harm's way, volunteering for Motor Torpedo Boat school in 1942. Becoming a "War Hero" would serve Joseph's purpose.

Before long, he was commanding a PT boat in the Pacific. Patrol, Torpedo boats were small, fast, and expendable vessels for short range oceanic scouting, armed with torpedoes and machine guns for cutting enemy supply lines and harassing enemy forces. Forty-three PT squadrons, each with twelve boats, were formed during World War II by the US Navy. PT boat duty was very dangerous, and the squadrons suffered an extremely high loss rate in the war.

PT-109

As the story goes, while in command of PT-109 in August 1943, he and his crew were surprised by a Japanese destroyer travelling at high speed; before anything could be done to avoid it, the PT boat was rammed and cut in half. Left floating in the sea with ten other surviving crew members, they avoided capture by swimming to a nearby island. However, since one of the crew was too badly burned to swim, Kennedy, who was injured himself, grabbed a strap of the man's life jacket, held it in his teeth and towed him three miles to land.

Kennedy on PT-109

In 1944 Joseph P. Kennedy Jr., JFK's older brother, was their father's choice to run for the presidency of the United States. Joseph Jr. died during the war when his plane blew up. Joseph Sr. picked John, the next in line for that challenge. From that point on, John's "positive image" became the goal of his father. The question became, "Did JFK do all for which he was credited?"

On March 1, 1945, Kennedy retired from the Navy Reserve because of physical disability and was honorably discharged with the full rank of lieutenant. When later asked how he became a war hero, Kennedy joked: "It was easy. They cut my PT boat in half."

Kennedy left the navy with serious injuries. After a brief stint in journalism, Kennedy represented a working-class Boston district in the US House of Representatives from 1947 to 1953. He was subsequently elected to the US Senate and served as the junior senator from Massachusetts from 1953 to 1960.

John married Jacqueline Bouvier on Sept. 12, 1953.

John and Jackie

He underwent several spinal operations over the next two years. Often absent from the Senate, he was at times critically ill and received Catholic last rites. In 1955, while recuperating from a back operation, he wrote *Profiles in Courage*, a book about US senators who risked their careers for their personal beliefs, for which he won the Pulitzer Prize for Biography in 1957. It was disappointing to learn that this work was co-written by his close adviser and speechwriter, Ted Sorensen, which was confirmed in Sorensen's 2008 autobiography. Seems that everything that John did to build a reputation of someone who would become the president was the plan of his father.

In the 1960 presidential election, Kennedy squared off against Richard Nixon in the first televised presidential debate in US history. During these programs, Nixon had an injured leg, "five o'clock shadow," and was perspiring profusely, making him look tense and uncomfortable. Conversely, Kennedy wore makeup and appeared relaxed, which helped the large television audience to view him as the winner.

JFK

The race between Kennedy and Nixon had been close all fall. The candidates were tied in a late August Gallup poll, and Kennedy took a three-point lead after his historic TV debate performances. But Nixon gained momentum heading into Election Day. And he cut Kennedy's lead to one percentage point in a poll taken four days before the election.

Kennedy defeated Nixon when votes were finally counted in the Electoral College, by a margin of 303 to 219. But in the popular vote, Kennedy won by just 112,000 votes out of sixty-eight million cast, or a margin on 0.2 percent.

Arguments persist to this day about vote-counting in two states, specifically Illinois (where Kennedy won by nine thousand votes) and Texas (where Kennedy won by forty-six votes). If Nixon had won those two states, he would have defeated Kennedy by two votes in the Electoral College.

John F. Kennedy was sworn in as the thirty-fifth president at noon on January 20, 1961. Kennedy was the first Catholic elected president.

John F. Kennedy becomes the President

In his inaugural address, Kennedy spoke of the need for all Americans to be active citizens, famously saying,

"Ask not what your country can do for you,

ask what you can do for your country."

JFK went to a private school and the headmaster was known to say: "As has often been said, the youth who loves his Alma Mater will always ask,

'Not what can she do for me, but what can I
do for her.'

JFK classmates sent letters to the school complaining that JFK plagiarized the headmaster. However, long before that, Oliver Wendell Holmes in a speech that he gave on May 30, 1884, said,

> "To recall what our country has done for each of us and ask ourselves what we can do for our country."

Like many Presidents before him, JFK learned the hard way why J. Edgar Hoover was FBI director for decades regardless of who occupied the Oval Office. The rumors are legendary. Hoover had embarrassing files on everybody in Washington, EVERYBODY!

JFK, Hoover, and Robert Kennedy

This was Hoover's job security, making him, in many regards, the most powerful man in the nation's capital. This was never more so than when the Kennedy brothers captured the White House.

Because Kennedy couldn't bring in his own FBI director, and be exposed to Hoover's assault, he named his younger brother, Robert as attorney general, making him Hoover's direct boss. Hoover hated Robert and his position of control. Hoover's files contained information about 1960 election fraud involving a pact between Joseph Kennedy and Chicago top mobster Sam Giancana that delivered Illinois to the Democrats. This confirmed that the election had been stolen. The mobsters became very displeased with the Kennedy's when AG Robert went after organized crime.

Hoover also knew about JFK's struggle with Addison's Disease, which he should have revealed as a Presidential candidate. And of course, his trump card, Pun intended, was the many sexual affairs the Kennedy brothers had. President Kennedy was the most vulnerable. His sexual adventures included a fling with Ellen Romansch, an east German Communist spy. Somehow, Hoover talked Kennedy into ending it. He also bedded Judith Campbell Exner, a knock-out brunette who also shared pillow talk with mafia strongman Sam Giancana, the same crime boss that helped get him elected.

Judith Exner

Ellen Romansch

Jayne Mansfield

Kennedy, according to his friends, considered no one off limits, including the wives, sisters, and mothers of his closest friends. His list of sexual conquests includes Hollywood actresses like *Marilyn Monroe, Jayne Mansfield, Gene Tierney, and* famous strippers like *Blaze Starr.* White House secretaries *Priscilla Weir and Jill Cowan*, who were referred to as "Fiddle" and "Faddle" were his regular partners. He had sex all over the White House, from the White House pool, where he regularly swam nude, to the closet of his bedroom, where he regularly put sex toys. Kennedy was not considered a great lover by friends, but rather a charming sex addict. "He reviled to close male friends; he would rarely kiss during sex because he wanted no personal relationships. He went more for quantity than quality," said Senator George Smathers, one of Kennedy's closest friends.

Gene Tierney

Fiddle and Faddle

Kennedy and Monroe

Whilst an intern at the White House, nineteen-year-old Mimi Alford lost her virginity to the President and engaged in an eighteen-month affair. Forty years later she revealed the details of their relationship, including that JFK took recreational drugs with her. JFK also successfully dared her to perform oral sex on his special assistant, Dave Powers, in the White House pool.

Blaze Starr   **Mimi**

Kennedy had a thing for blondes. Everyone knows about his affair with Marilyn Monroe; yet not as many know about Mary Pinchot Meyer, another beautiful, curvy blonde who gave JFK pause. Like Monroe, Meyer too died young, murdered on a towpath in Georgetown, Washington, DC, in broad daylight on October 12, 1964. More than fifty years later, her murder remains unsolved but the holes in the story, her close CIA ties, and her affair with JFK have led many to believe that Meyer's life ended with a professional hit. A curiously involved, ornate, and clumsy hit but a hit, nonetheless.

Mary

Cuba became a point of contention during the Cold War between the Soviet Union and the United States.

During the Eisenhower administration a plan to overthrow Fidel Castro's regime in Cuba was created by the CIA. In April 1961, Kennedy continued with and authorized the attempt to overthrow the Cuban government of Fidel Castro in the Invasion. Unbeknownst to the CIA trainers, sprinkled amongst the recruits being trained were double agents, working in tandem for Castro, sharing the intelligence that they collected on the upcoming invasion.

As the number of days till the invasion shortened, Kennedy's concern that the operation would not remain a secret from the public. He was adamant the hand of the US Government remain hidden at all costs. Kennedy thought changing the invasion site from Trinidad would make future deniability of US involvement more plausible, so he gave the CIA four days to come up with a new one. A month before the operation was set to get underway, the landing location changed from Trinidad to the Bay of Pigs.

Changing the plan at this late date was a big mistake.

Kennedy also made the decision to cancel the air strikes set to destroy the remaining fleet of Cuban bombers. The decision was so last minute that the brigade pilots were sitting on the runway, taxied in position for takeoff when they were told to stand down, another mistake which made the invasion close to impossible. The exiles went into battle believing that America had their back. Kennedy refused to authorize any direct air support. When America backed out on suppling artillery and weapons to the exiles, they were completely outnumbered by Castro's forces. Members of the brigade either surrendered or returned home. When all was said and done, more than seventy-five percent of the CIA trained brigade ended up in Cuban prisons.

The "Bay of Pigs" failure was devastating for Kennedy.

I was personally very disappointed with the president's handling of the whole situation. I felt as though Castro and Communism won and America lost the battle. The whole affair caused Castro to hate Kennedy and America. It was common belief that Castro had a strong desire to get even with Kennedy. Shortly afterwards it was discovered that Soviet missile bases had been set-up in Cuba. The then called, "Cuban Missile Crisis," the threat of a global thermonuclear conflict that nearly resulted in WWIII was at hand. After the embarrassing "Bay of Pigs" debacle the pressure was on.

On October 22, Kennedy decided on a naval quarantine. He dispatched a message to Khrushchev and announced the decision on national TV. The US Navy would stop and inspect all Soviet ships arriving off Cuba, beginning October 24. The Organization of American States gave unanimous support to the removal of the missiles. The president exchanged two sets of letters with Khrushchev, to no avail. United Nations Secretary General U Thant requested both parties to reverse their decisions and enter a cooling-off period. Khrushchev agreed, but **Kennedy did not**.

One Soviet-flagged ship was stopped and boarded. On October 28, Khrushchev agreed to dismantle the missile sites, subject to UN inspections. *The U.S. publicly promised never to invade Cuba* and privately agreed to remove its Jupiter missiles from Italy and Turkey, which were by then obsolete and had been supplanted by submarines equipped with UGM-27 Polaris missiles. The US promise was not honored.

A document from the United States Department of State confirms **Operation Mongoose**, was a project aimed to help Cuba overthrow the Communist regime. This included its leader Fidel Castro, and it aimed for a revolt to take place in Cuba by October 1962. US policymakers wanted to see a new government with which the United States could live in peace. Mongoose never occurred.

Kennedy signed the first nuclear weapons treaty in 1963.

During the summer of 1962, Kennedy had a secret taping system set up in the Oval Office, most likely to aid his future memoir. It recorded many conversations with Kennedy and his Cabinet members, including those in relation to the "Cuban Missile Crisis." This taping system became a big problem for Nixon in the Watergate break-in trial.

In one of his first presidential acts, Kennedy asked Congress to create the Peace Corps. His brother-in-law, Sargent Shriver, was its first director. Kennedy presided over the establishment of the Peace Corps, Alliance for Progress with Latin America, and the continuation of the Apollo program with the goal of landing a man on the Moon before 1970.

John F. Kennedy, was assassinated on Friday, November 22, 1963, at 12:30 p.m. CST in Dallas, Texas, while riding in a presidential motorcade through Dealey Plaza. Kennedy was riding with his wife Jackie, Texas Governor John Connally, and Connally's wife Nellie when he was fatally shot by Lee Harvey Oswald. Oswald shot and killed Kennedy from a sixth floor window of the Texas School Book Depository. About forty-five minutes after assassinating Kennedy, Oswald shot and killed Dallas police officer J. D. Tippit on a local street. He then slipped into a movie theater, where he was arrested for Tippit's murder. Oswald was charged with the assassination of President Kennedy, but he denied responsibility for the killing, claiming that he was a "patsy." Governor Connally was seriously wounded in the attack. The motorcade rushed to Parkland

Memorial Hospital, where Kennedy was pronounced dead. Governor Connally recovered.

Seventy minutes after the initial shooting. Oswald was charged under Texas state law with the murder of Kennedy and that of police officer J.D. Tippit. At 11:21 a.m. November 24, 1963, as live television cameras were covering his transfer from the Dallas Police Department's city jail to the county jail. Oswald was fatally shot in the basement of Dallas Police Headquarters by Dallas nightclub operator Jack Ruby. Oswald was taken to Parkland Memorial Hospital, where he soon died.

Lee Harvey Oswald

Oswald lived a very troubled life. He was placed in juvenile detention at the age of twelve for truancy, during which time he was assessed by a psychiatrist as "emotionally disturbed," due to a lack of normal family life. After attending twenty-two schools in his youth, he quit repeatedly, and finally when he was seventeen, joined the Marines. Oswald was court-martialed twice while in the Marines and jailed. He was honorably released from active duty in the Marine Corps into the reserve, then promptly flew to Europe and defected to the Soviet Union in October 1959.

Ruby kills Oswald

He lived in Minsk, Byelorussia, married a Russian woman named Marina, and had a daughter. In June 1962, he returned to the United States with his wife, and eventually settled in Dallas, where their second daughter was born.

Jacob Leon Rubenstein, alias, "Jack Ruby" was an American nightclub owner who fatally shot Oswald while he was in police custody.

Jack Ruby

Ruby made his way into the basement of the Dallas Police Department via a stairway accessible from an alleyway. At 11:21 a.m. CST, while authorities were escorting Oswald through the police basement to an armored car that was to take him to the nearby county jail, Ruby stepped out from a crowd of reporters with his .38 Colt Cobra revolver aimed at Oswald and fired a single round, mortally wounding him. The bullet entered Oswald's left side in the front part of the abdomen and caused damage to his spleen, stomach, aorta, kidney, liver, diaphragm, and eleventh rib before coming to rest on his right side. Oswald made a cry of anguish, and his manacled hands clutched at his abdomen as he writhed with pain, and he slumped to the concrete paving, where he moaned several times. Police detective Billy Combest suddenly recognized Ruby and exclaimed: "Jack, you son of a bitch!" Ruby was immediately subdued by police as a moaning Oswald was carried back into the basement level jail office. Combest asked Oswald, "Do you have anything you want to tell us now?" Oswald shook his head. He lost consciousness shortly thereafter. Taken by ambulance to the same hospital where President Kennedy had been pronounced dead two days earlier, Lee Harvey Oswald died at 1:07 p.m.

A Dallas jury found Ruby guilty of murdering Oswald, and he was sentenced to death. Ruby's conviction was later appealed, and he was granted a new trial. However, as the date for his new trial was being set, Ruby became ill in prison and died of a pulmonary embolism from lung cancer on January 3, 1967.

Conspiracy questions as to whether Kennedy was killed by Chicago top mobster Sam Giancana or Fidel Castro followed. Ten months of investigation, by the Warren Commission concluded that Oswald had acted entirely alone when he killed Kennedy, and that Ruby had acted alone in killing Oswald.

Robert Francis Kennedy (November 20, 1925 – June 6, 1968), also referred to by his initials **RFK** or by the nickname **Bobby**, was an American lawyer and politician who served as the sixty-forth United States Attorney General from January 1961 to September 1964, and as a US Senator from New York from January 1965 until June 1968. He was, like his brothers John and Edward, a prominent member of the Democrat Party and has come to be viewed by some historians as an icon of modern American liberalism. In 1968, Kennedy became a leading candidate for the Democrat nomination for the presidency by appealing to poor, Black Americans, Hispanic, Catholic, and young voters. Shortly after winning the California primary around midnight on June 5, 1968, Kennedy was mortally wounded when shot with a pistol by Sirhan-

Sirhan, a twenty-four-year-old Palestinian, allegedly in retaliation for his support of Israel following the 1967 Six-Day War. Kennedy died twenty-five hours later. Sirhan was arrested, tried, and convicted, though Kennedy's assassination, like his brother's, continues to be the subject of widespread analysis and numerous conspiracy theories.

RFK

In an interview with Life Magazine a week after her husband's death, Jackie described John's love for **Camelot,** a musical based on the popular Arthurian novel "The Once and Future King." She noted that the president enjoyed playing a recording of the musical's title song, which featured the line, *don't let it be forgot, that once there was a spot, for one brief, shining moment, that was known as Camelot.* After quoting the lyrics, Jackie went on to say, "There will be great presidents again, but there will never be another Camelot." The interview proved hugely popular, and *"Camelot"* soon became shorthand for the *myth and glamour* of the Kennedy administration. She was the first to refer to the Kennedy administration as "Camelot."

"JFK was a serial womanizer. He spent more time chasing women than running the country. He was my favorite back then but, was disappointing."

CHAPTER NINE

Lyndon Baines Johnson

Lyndon was born on August 27, 1908, near Stonewall, Texas, in a small farmhouse on the Pedernales River. He was the eldest of five children born to Samuel Ealy Johnson Jr. and Rebekah Baines.

Lyndon at age seven with his trademark cowboy hat

In school, Lyndon was extremely talkative. He was elected president of his eleventh-grade class. He graduated in 1924 from Johnson City High School, where he participated in public speaking, and played baseball. In 1926 Lyndon enrolled at what is now Texas State University. He worked his way through school and participated in debate and campus politics. He edited the school newspaper, the *College Star*. His college years honed his skills of persuasion and political organization.

After **Richard M. Kleberg** won a 1931 special election to represent Texas in the United States House of Representatives, he appointed Lyndon as his legislative secretary. Kleberg had little interest in performing the day-to-day duties of a congressman, instead delegating them to Lyndon. Lyndon, still extremely talkative, was elected speaker of the "Little Congress," a group of Congressional aides. In this position he became friends with many Congressmen, newspapermen, and lobbyists.

On November 17, 1934, Lyndon married Claudia Alta Taylor, of Karnack, Texas. Lyndon met her after he had attended Georgetown University Law Center for several months. When she was born, Claudia's nurse said, *"She's as puny as a lady bird,"* and the nickname stuck. During his first date with Lady Bird, Lyndon asked her to marry him; on a later date, she agreed. They had two daughters, Lynda Bird, born in 1944, and Luci Baines, born in 1947. Johnson gave all his children names with the "LBJ" initials; even his dog was Little Beagle Johnson. His home was the LBJ Ranch; his initials were on his cufflinks, ashtrays, and clothes.

Lady Bird Johnson

Lyndon had his harem of women. Although, he was much better at keeping his extramarital affairs more discreet than his predecessor, JFK. One of his many sexual partners became pregnant in 1950, prior to him becoming president. Her name was Madeline Brown, and she gave birth to LBJ's son who was named Steven. Though Steven was not given the "LBJ" initials, Johnson did take care of Madeline and his son financially, both before and after Steven was born. The illicit affair lasted for twenty-one years, and Johnson set her up in an apartment for their discreet rendezvous.

Madeline and Steven

During his marriage, Lyndon had affairs with multiple women, including Alice Marsh Glass who assisted him politically. Lyndon seemed unconcerned with how his long-term affair with Alice Glass might affect Lady Bird. Lyndon maintained his on-and-off relationship with Glass between 1939 and the early years of his presidency. His relationship with Glass was risky because she also was romantically involved with one of his big donors.

Alice Glass Marsh

It's clear that Lady Bird knew about Glass and the other women Lyndon slept with. When Lady Bird died in 2007, *The Guardian* noted in her obituary: "Lyndon was so casual in his affairs with Alice Glass and his congressional colleague Helen Gahagan Douglas that Lady Bird was openly humiliated." This isn't surprising considering that Lyndon was known for exposing his genitals and bragging that he'd had sex with more women than JFK.

Along with the rest of the nation, Johnson was appalled by the threat of possible Soviet domination of space flight implied by the launch of the first artificial earth satellite Sputnik 1. He then used his influence to ensure passage of the 1958 National Aeronautics and Space Act, which established the civilian space agency **NASA.**

A five-pack-cigarette-per-day smoker, Johnson suffered a near-fatal heart attack on July 2, 1955, at age forty-six. He abruptly gave up smoking.

Johnson's success in the Senate rendered him a potential Democratic presidential candidate; he had been the "favorite son" candidate of the Texas delegation at the Party's national convention in 1956, and appeared to be in a strong position to run for the 1960 nomination.

Johnson underestimated Kennedy's endearing qualities of charm and intelligence, as compared to his reputation as the cruder wheeler-dealer. Johnson attempted to capitalize on Kennedy's youth, his poor health, and his failure to take a position regarding Joseph McCarthy. He had formed a "Stop Kennedy" coalition, but it proved a failure. Tip O'Neil was a representative from Kennedy's home state of Massachusetts at that time, and he recalled that Johnson approached him at the convention and said, "Tip, I know you have to support Kennedy at the start, but I'd like to have you with me on the second ballot." O'Neill replied, "Senator, there's not going to be any second ballot."

As a young man at the time, I vividly remember that Jack Kennedy believed he could not win the presidency running against Nixon without the support of the Southern Democrats, most of whom supported Lyndon Johnson. Even though Jack's brother Robert and many other democrat leaders opposed Lyndon, Jack offered him the vice-presidential nomination after he was nominated, and Lyndon accepted.

Tip O'Neill

Congressman Tip O'Neill recalled that the Kennedy men "had such a dislike for Johnson that they didn't even try to hide it. They took great pride in snubbing him."

Kennedy appointed Johnson Chairman of the National Aeronautics and Space Council. The Soviets beat the United States with the first manned spaceflight in April 1961, and Kennedy gave Johnson the task of creating a program that would allow the United States to beat the Soviets to the moon.

Lyndon Baines Johnson takes oath of office on Air Force One.

Lyndon Baines Johnson automatically became the thirty-sixth president of the United States upon Kennedys death. LBJ was sworn in on *Air Force One* in Dallas after Kennedy's death on November 22, 1963, by Judge Sarah Hughes as Lady Bird and Jackie looked on.

At this time, I was sitting in a marketing meeting at the Beltone Hearing Aid Company in Chicago when in walked a messenger who brought us the news that President Kennedy had just been shot while riding in convertible in Dallas, Texas. If you ask anyone who was an adult at the time of Kennedy's assignation where they were at the time it happened, I am sure they will remember the moment.

On November 27, 1963, the new president delivered his "Let Us Continue" speech to a joint session of Congress, saying that "No memorial oration or eulogy could more eloquently honor President Kennedy's memory than the earliest possible passage of the Civil Rights Bill for which he fought so long." The wave of national grief following the assassination gave enormous momentum to Johnson's promise to carry out Kennedy's plans and his policy of seizing Kennedy's legacy to give momentum to his legislative agenda.

Barely seven months after addressing Congress, Johnson would sign the Civil Rights Act of 1964, which prohibited discrimination on the basis of race, color, religion, sex, or national origin, banned segregation and provided for the integration of schools and other public facilities. That Johnson was the president to pass such a historic bill seemed ironic. *As a congressman, he voted against every single civil rights bill that ever made it to the floor between 1937 and 1956.* Even more paradoxically, as a Southern man of his time, Johnson used racist language, even as he smashed Jim Crow laws across the South.

Johnson wanted a catchy slogan for the 1964 campaign to describe his proposed domestic agenda for 1965. "The Great Society." Johnson won the presidency by a landslide with 61.05 percent of the vote, making it the highest ever share of the popular vote.

In his first State of the Union address, Johnson declared an "unconditional war" on poverty in the United States, announcing that "Our aim is not only to relieve the symptoms of poverty, but to cure it and, above all, to prevent it."

He spearheaded legislation creating **Medicare** and **Medicaid**, expanding Social Security, making the food stamps program permanent and establishing Job Corps, the VISTA program, the federal work-study program, the **Head Start program,** and Title I subsidies for poor school districts. Though the war on poverty is still far from being won, the programs put in place as part of Johnson's "Great Society" did succeed in reducing economic hardships for millions of Americans, and many are still in place today.

In 1965, he achieved passage of a second civil rights bill, called the Voting Rights Act, which outlawed discrimination in voting, thus allowing millions of southern blacks to vote for the first time.

Thurgood Marshall

In 1967 Johnson nominated civil rights attorney **Thurgood Marshall** to be the first African American justice of the Supreme Court. In 1968, Johnson signed the Civil Rights Act of 1968, which provided for equal housing opportunities regardless of race, creed, or national origin. The impetus for the law's passage came from the 1966 Chicago Open Housing Movement, the April 4, 1968, assassination of Martin Luther King Jr., and the civil unrest across the country following King's death.

During Johnson's years in office, national poverty declined significantly, with the percentage of Americans living below the poverty line dropping from 23 percent to 12 percent.

In 1965 Johnson turned his focus to hospital insurance for the aged under Social Security. The key player in initiating this program named **Medicare**. The Medicare bill passed Congress on July 28. Medicare now covers tens of millions of Americans.

Major riots in black neighborhoods caused a series of "long hot summers." They started with a violent disturbance in the Harlem riots in 1964, and the Watts district of Los Angeles in 1965, and extended to 1971. The momentum for the advancement of civil rights came to a sudden halt in the summer of 1965, with the riots in Watts. After thirty-four people were killed and thirty-five million dollars (equivalent to $287.43 million in 2020) in property was damaged, the public feared an expansion of the violence to other cities, and so the appetite for additional programs in LBJ's agenda was lost.

At Kennedy's death, there were sixteen thousand American military personnel stationed in Vietnam supporting South Vietnam in the war against North Vietnam.

By the end of 1964, there were approximately twenty-three thousand military personnel in South Vietnam; U.S. casualties for 1964 totaled 1,278.

By the middle of 1965, the total U.S. ground forces in Vietnam were increased to eighty-two thousand, or by 150 percent. By October 1965, there were over two hundred thousand troops deployed in Vietnam.

Public and political impatience with the war began to emerge in the spring of 1966, and Johnson's approval ratings reached a new low of 41 percent. Sen. Richard Russell, Chairman of the Armed Services Committee, reflected the national mood in June 1966 when he declared it was time to **get it over or get out.** Johnson responded by saying to the press, "We are trying to provide the maximum deterrence that we can to communist aggression with a minimum of cost." By the middle of 1967, nearly **seventy thousand** Americans had been killed or wounded in the war.

As casualties mounted and success seemed further away than ever, Johnson's popularity plummeted. College students and others protested, burned draft cards, and chanted, "Hey, hey, LBJ, how many kids did you kill today?" Johnson could scarcely travel anywhere without facing protests, and was not allowed by the Secret Service to attend the 1968 Democratic National Convention, where thousands of hippies, yippies, Black Panthers, and other opponents of Johnson's policies both in Vietnam and in the ghettos converged to protest. Thus by 1968, the public was polarized, with the "hawks" rejecting Johnson's refusal to continue the war indefinitely, and the "doves" rejecting his current war policies.

Ironically, Walter Cronkite of CBS News, voted the nation's "most trusted person" in February, opined on the air that the conflict was deadlocked and that additional fighting would change nothing. Johnson reacted, saying,

Cronkite and Roy

"If I've lost Cronkite, I've lost middle America." Indeed, demoralization about the war was everywhere; 26 percent then approved of Johnson's handling of Vietnam; 63 percent disapproved. Johnson agreed to increase the troop level by twenty-two thousand, despite a recommendation from the Joint Chiefs for ten times that number. By March 1968, Johnson was secretly desperate for an honorable way out of the war. Clark Clifford, the new defense secretary, described the war as "a loser" and proposed to "cut losses and get out." On March 31, Johnson spoke to the nation of "Steps to Limit the War in Vietnam." He then announced an immediate unilateral halt to the bombing of North Vietnam and announced his intention to seek out peace talks anywhere at any time. At the close of his speech he also announced, *"I shall not seek, and I will not accept, the nomination of my party for another term as your President."*

Johnson continued the FBI's wiretapping of Martin Luther King Jr. that had been previously authorized by the Kennedy administration under Attorney General Robert F. Kennedy. As a result of listening to the FBI's tapes, remarks on King's extra-marital activities were made by several prominent officials, including Johnson, who once said that King was a "hypocritical preacher." This was despite the fact that Johnson himself had multiple extramarital affairs.

Johnson had become more worried about his failing health and was concerned that he might not live through another four-year term. In 1967, he secretly commissioned an actuarial study that accurately predicted he would die at sixty-four. On Inauguration Day (January 20, 1969), Johnson saw Nixon sworn in, then got on the plane to fly back to Texas. When the front door of the plane closed, Johnson pulled out a cigarette—his first cigarette he had smoked since his heart attack in 1955. One of his daughters pulled it out of his mouth and said, "Daddy, what are you doing? You're going to kill yourself." He took it back and said, "I've now raised you, girls. I've now been president. "Now it's my time!" From that point on, he went into a very self-destructive spiral.

LBJ, "Now it's my time!"

His heart condition rapidly worsened and surgery was recommended, so Johnson flew to Houston to consult with heart specialist Dr. Michael DeBakey, where he learned his condition was terminal. Johnson recorded an hour-long television interview with newsman Walter Cronkite at his ranch on January 12, 1973, in which he discussed his legacy, particularly about the civil rights movement.

Ten days later, at approximately 3:39 p.m. Central Time on January 22, 1973, Johnson suffered a massive heart attack in his bedroom. He managed to telephone the Secret Service agents on the ranch, who found him still holding the telephone receiver, unconscious and not breathing. Cardiologist and army colonel Dr. George McGranahan pronounced him dead on arrival. He was sixty-four years old.

"Like JFK, LBJ was a serial womanizer and spent a lot of time chasing women."

CHAPTER TEN

Richard Milhous Nixon

Richard Milhous Nixon was born on January 9, 1913, in Yorba Linda, California. He was the second of five sons of Francis Anthony Nixon, who struggled to earn a living running a grocery store and gas station, and his wife, Hannah Milhous Nixon. Richard absorbed his parents' discontent with their working-class circumstances and developed a strong sense of ambition.

Richard

He attended Whittier College, where he excelled as a debater and was elected president of the student body before graduating in 1934. Three years later, he earned a law degree from Duke University, where he was head of the student bar association and graduated near the top of his class. After Duke, he returned to Whittier, California, and began working as an attorney.

Pat

In 1940, Nixon married Thelma Catherine "Pat" Ryan, whom he met while participating in a local theater group. The couple had two daughters, Patricia and Julie. When America entered World War II, Richard joined the US Navy and served as an operations officer in the Pacific.

Following the war, Richard launched his political career in 1946 when he defeated a five-term Democratic incumbent to represent his California district in the US House of Representatives. As a congressman, Nixon served on the House Un-American Activities Committee and rose to national prominence by leading a controversial investigation of Alger Hiss, a well-regarded former State Department official who was accused of spying for the Soviet Union in the late 1930s.

Nixon was re-elected to Congress in 1948 and two years later, in 1950, won a seat in the US Senate.

In July of 1952, Richard Nixon was nominated as the vice-presidential candidate by the delegates attending the Republican National Convention. General Dwight D. Eisenhower was the presidential nominee.

It was well known that the Nixon's were not wealthy, and even in the 1950s, campaigning was costly. Within a couple of months of the nomination, a news story broke about "Nixon's Secret Fund." The report focused on the belief that campaign donors were buying influence with Nixon by having set up a secret fund to cover his personal expenses.

The accusations were denied by those representing the Republican ticket. Campaign representatives said they had ordered an independent review and the claims about the fund were false. The fund existed but the money was used exclusively for campaign expenses.

The negative stories, however, did not die down. Eisenhower was being pressured to dump Nixon from the ticket. In a last-ditch attempt to save himself, Nixon opted to appear on national television. He addressed the public in a thirty-minute speech. He spoke from behind a desk with Pat sitting a bit behind him and to the side.

Nixon began by revealing his personal financial situation and talked about the fact that the independent review found him blameless. He talked of many things, including Pat's cloth coat (as opposed to a mink coat that a well-to-do woman of the day might wear). At that reference, the camera pulled back to reveal Pat listening solicitously.

He then continued, talking about a recent gift that had been given to the family:

"One other thing I probably should tell you because if we don't, they'll probably be saying this about me, too, we did get something –a gift— after the [Senate] election. A man down in Texas heard Pat on the radio mention the fact that our two youngsters would like to have a dog. And believe it or not, the day before we left on this campaign trip, we got a message from Union Station in Baltimore saying they had a package for us. We went down to get it."

Nixon and Checkers

"You know what it was? It was a little Cocker spaniel dog in a crate that he'd sent all the way from Texas. Black-and-white spotted. And our little girl—Tricia, the six-year-old—named it Checkers. And you know the kids, like all kids, love the dog and I just want to say this right now, that regardless of what they say about it, we're going to keep it."

The speech, now known as the "Checkers speech," was heard by a very sizable audience—approximately sixty million Americans.

The speech prompted a huge public outpouring of support for Nixon. Eisenhower and Nixon won the election that November.

In 1960, Vice President Richard M. Nixon ran for President of the United States. His opponent was Senator John F. Kennedy and Nixon lost.

On November 5, 1968, Richard Milhous Nixon was elected as the thirty-seventh President of the United States.

Nixon takes oath of office

He defeated Vice President Hubert Humphrey and Alabama Governor George Wallace in the general election.

On July 18, 1969, **Senator Edward M. Kennedy** left a party on Chappaquiddick at 11:15 p.m. Friday, with a young companion Mary Jo Kopechne. Mary Jo served on Robert Kennedy's 1968 presidential campaign. Edward maintained that his intent was to take Mary Jo to the ferry landing so she could return to Edgartown.

Senator Edward Kennedy and Mary Jo

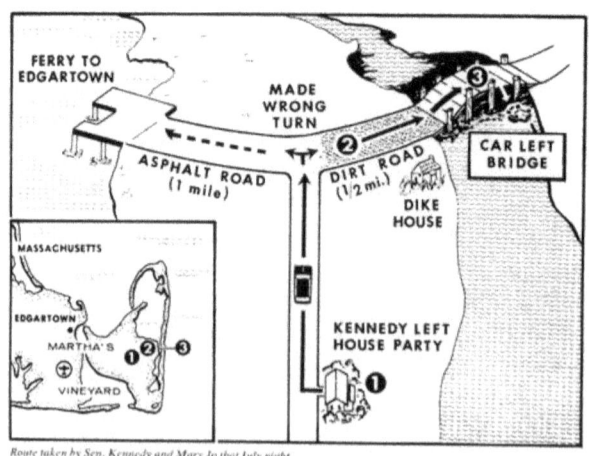

Think about it, the Kennedys spent thirty years on Chappaquiddick, and this tiny island only had one main road. Stay on the paved road, turn left to the ferry, or turn right on to a dirt road leading to the secret hide-a-way where people go to play. I personally didn't believe they were headed for the ferry as Edward stated. Mary Jo left her purse and car keys at the party house. The Kennedy Oldsmobile went off the bridge into the deep water below. After Kennedy crawled out of the submerged car, he left the scene of the accident and walked to the ferry landing, dove into the channel, swam the five hundred feet across to Edgartown, and returned to his hotel room, where he removed his wet clothes and collapsed on his bed. Kennedy did not report the incident until 9:50 a.m. the next day. By then he was sober. Scuba diver John Farrar, who recovered Kopechne's body from the submerged car, believed that Kopechne died from suffocation, rather than from drowning or from the impact of the overturned vehicle, based upon the posture in which he found the body in the well of the back seat of the car, where an air pocket would have formed. Rigor mortis was apparent, her hands were clasping the back seat, and her face was turned upward. Bob Molla, an inspector for the Massachusetts Registry of Motor Vehicles who investigated the crash at the time, said that parts of the roof and the trunk appeared to be dry. Farrar publicly asserted that Kopechne would have probably survived if a timelier rescue attempt had been conducted. Farrar believed that Kopechne "lived for at least two hours down there."

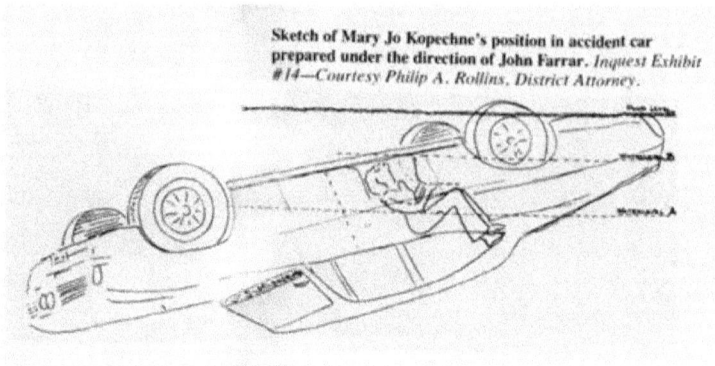

Sketch of Mary Jo Kopechne's position in accident car prepared under the direction of John Farrar. *Inquest Exhibit #14—Courtesy Philip A. Rollins, District Attorney.*

Kennedy's wife Joan was pregnant at the time of the Chappaquiddick incident. She was confined to bed because of two previous miscarriages, but she attended Kopechne's funeral and stood beside her husband in court. Soon after, she suffered a third miscarriage, which she blamed on the Chappaquiddick incident. Kennedy in a speech asked the people of Massachusetts to decide whether he should resign. NBC newsman John Chancellor compared his speech to Richard Nixon's 1952 Checkers speech.

The people of Massachusetts forgave Kennedy, **I did not!**

My attitude about the Kennedy's changed. I believed Edward Kennedy partied, got drunk and was responsible for a young girl's death.

On July 20, 1969, Nixon made the longest long-distance phone call in history, as astronaut's Neil Armstrong and Buzz Aldrin took **mankind's first steps on the Moon.**

President Richard Nixon entered office in 1969 with Chief Justice Earl Warren having announced his retirement from **Supreme Court of the United States** the previous year. Nixon appointed Warren E. Burger to replace Earl Warren, and during his time in office appointed three other members of the Supreme Court: Associate Justices Harry Blackmun, Lewis F. Powell, and William Rehnquist.

Nixon also nominated Clement Haynsworth and G. Harrold Carswell for the vacancy that was ultimately filled by Blackmun, but the nominations were rejected by the United States Senate. Nixon's failed Supreme Court nominations were the first since Herbert Hoover's nomination of John J. Parker was rejected by the Senate. By many standards Richard Milhouse Nixon was a great president. As our leader he gave of himself as he moved unafraid to build on our everlasting freedom.

On July 15, 1971, Nixon announced that he had been invited to the People's Republic of China, ending a quarter of a century of hostility between the United States and China. In his trip to China in February 1962, Nixon met with Chairman Mao Zedong and Premier Zhou Enlia and set forth a plan for peaceful relations through the Shanghai Communique. Nixon called it,

"The week that changed the world."

Late May 1972, during Nixon's official visit to Tehran, Iran, a "Marxist terrorist group" named People's Mujahedin of Iran blew up a bomb at Reza Shah's mausoleum, where Nixon was scheduled to attend a ceremony just forty-five minutes after the explosion. This may have been the earliest known attempt on the president's life by an Islamic extremist.

February 22, 1974, Samuel Byck planned to kill Nixon by crashing a commercial airliner into the White House. He hijacked a DC-9 at Baltimore-Washington International Airport after killing a Maryland Aviation Administration police officer, and was told that it could not take off with the wheel blocks still in place. After he shot both pilots (one later died), an officer named Charles "Butch" Troyer shot Byck through the plane's door window. He survived long enough to kill himself by shooting.

The United States, South Vietnam, Viet Cong, and North Vietnam formally signed an agreement on January 27, 1973, ending the Vietnam War.

Nixon was very smart with an IQ of 131 and yet he made a very stupid un-needed and fatal mistake. He was well on his way to winning his presidential re-election in 1972, he needed no help, and yet he authorized a shameful act against his opponent, George McGovern. The scandal began when five burglars broke into the Democratic Party's National Committee offices in May 1972. The offices were located at the Watergate office-apartment-hotel complex one of Washington DC's finest buildings. Top secret papers were taken, and microphones were installed to gather further information.

The wiretaps failed to work properly, however, so on June 17th the group of five burglars returned to the Watergate building. As the prowlers were breaking into the office with a new microphone system, a security guard noticed someone had taped over several of the building's door locks. The guard called the police, who arrived just in time to catch them red-handed.

The Watergate Complex

Attorney General John Mitchel was in California campaigning for Nixon when he received a call alerting him that five men had been arrested at the Watergate complex for the break-in he was said to have authorized. John headed for Washington, leaving his wife Martha behind at the hotel, reportedly under the watch of security aide and former FBI agent Stephen King. While John was away, Martha read the news and saw photos of one of the captured burglars, James McCord. Martha recognized McCord since he was a former CIA officer and security consultant for the re-election campaign who had recently been Martha's personal security guard. Martha made late-night calls to the press alerting them to what she knew. Martha's nickname in Washington was the "Mouth of the South."

It was not immediately clear that the burglars were connected to the president, though suspicions were raised when detectives found copies of the re-election committee's White House phone number among the burglars' belongings.

Washington Post reporters Bob Woodward and Carl Bernstein had begun to suspect that there was a larger scheme afoot.

In August, Nixon gave a speech in which he swore that his White House staff was not involved in the break-in. Most voters believed him, and in November 1972 the president was re-elected in a landslide victory.

Then, Nixon and his aides hatched a plan to instruct the Central Intelligence Agency (CIA) to impede the FBI's investigation of the crime. This was a more serious crime than the break-in. It was an abuse of presidential power and a deliberate obstruction of justice.

At the same time, some of the conspirators began to crack under the pressure of the cover-up. Anonymous whistleblower "Deep Throat" who met with *Washington Post* reporter Carl Bernstein in the lower level of a parking garage and spoke in a very deep voice and provided key information and details about the involvement of President Richard Nixon's administration in the Watergate scandal. *(In 2005, thirty-one years after Nixon's resignation and eleven years after Nixon's death, a family attorney stated that former FBI Associate Director Mark Felt was Deep Throat.)* Woodward and Bernstein confirmed the Whistleblower's claim. The problem Woodward and Bernstein had was they had no proof that connected the Watergate break-in directly to Nixon. And then came the phone conversation with **Kenny Dahlberg**. Captured on the Oval Office secret taping system that JFK had installed, President Nixon asked on

June 23, "Who the hell is Kenneth Dahlberg?" Without Kenneth Dahlberg, Nixon might not have become ensnared in the Watergate scandal. Dahlberg's name was on the twenty-five-thousand-dollar cashier's check that had been deposited in the bank account of one of the burglars, Bernard L. Barker. The money was to help pay for the burglar's expenses. Woodward has called the Dahlberg check the "connective tissue" that turned what they thought was a story about a minor crime into one of historic dimensions.

Dahlberg

In World War II, Dahlberg was a triple ace fighter pilot. He shot down fifteen German planes. He himself was shot down and captured three times. He escaped twice, once by riding a bike, dressed as a woman, for forty miles to Allied lines. His many decorations included the Distinguished Service Cross, the army's second-highest award for bravery. Listed as "killed in action" while a prisoner of war, he didn't receive his medals until eighteen years after the war had ended. Dahlberg was head of Midwestern fund-raising for the Nixon re-election campaign. A friend of his, Dwayne Andreas wanted to contribute to the Republicans but wanted to conceal it from another friend, Democrat Hubert Humphrey. Dahlberg converted the twenty-five thousand dollars into a cashier's check written in his name.

At an International Hearing Aid convention, Kenny and I discussed the Watergate affair. He told me that when he received a call from the *Washington Post* reporter, he hung up on him. He then decided it might become a problem, so he called the reporter back and told him that he had sent the check to Maurice Stans. Stans was the National Finance Chairman for the Nixon campaign. Bernstein and Woodward now knew that the money received by the men who burglarized the Democratic Party's National Committee offices at the Watergate Hotel came from the top.

White House counsel John Dean testified before a grand jury that Nixon had secretly taped every conversation that took place in the Oval Office. Nixon's lawyers argued that the president's executive privilege allowed him to keep the tapes to himself. Eventually, Nixon agreed to surrender some of the tapes, which had several gaps of about eighteen minutes.

Nixon's Vice President Spiro Agnew is perhaps most well-known for the end of his career. He was forced to resign from office after being charged with extortion, bribery, conspiracy and pleading no contest to income-tax evasion in 1973. Agnew was replaced by **Gerald Ford**.

With all of Richard Nixon's immense political skills, intelligence, ability, and achievements, he allowed his uncontrollable paranoia to destroy him. In the last days of July

1974, most of President Nixon's aides concluded that Nixon's position was untenable, and that resignation was imminent.

When Secretary of State Henry Kissinger answered the president's summons on the evening of August 7, 1974, he found that Nixon was nearly drunk, sitting in a darkened room, and lost in thought. The president would drink scotch and get drunk quickly; he was famously unable to handle his low tolerance for alcohol very well.

Nixon urged the diplomat to stay on as Secretary of State and provide Gerald Ford with the same service he had provided him. Sitting there in the smallest room of the White House, Nixon asked Kissinger about how he would be remembered. Although he had made mistakes, he felt that he had accomplished great things for his country. Nixon was worried that his legacy would be Watergate and resignation, but he desperately wanted to be thought of as a president who achieved peace. Kissinger insisted that Nixon would get the credit he deserved.

Henry Kissinger

President Nixon started crying ashamed by the disgrace he had brought to his country. Nixon was a man who never wore his Quaker religion on his sleeve. He turned to Kissinger and asked him if he would pray with him. Despite being Jewish, Kissinger felt he had no choice but to kneel with the president as Nixon prayed for peace, both for his country and for himself. Kissinger helped Nixon up to his feet and the men shared another drink, talking openly about what role Nixon could have in the future as a former president.

Before leaving the White House on August 9th, 1974, Nixon made an impromptu speech to White House employees in the East Room of the mansion. He talked about his family, his achievements, and his appreciation for the people who worked in his administration. He rambled at times, and he was clearly saddened by the situation. And, towards the end of his speech, he said,

> "Always give your best, never get discouraged, never be petty; always remember, others may hate you, but those who hate you don't win unless you hate them, and then you destroy yourself."

> THE WHITE HOUSE
> WASHINGTON
>
> August 9, 1974
>
> Dear Mr. Secretary:
>
> I hereby resign the Office of President of the United States.
>
> Sincerely,
>
> *[signature]*
>
> The Honorable Henry A. Kissinger
> The Secretary of State
> Washington, D. C. 20520

After Nixon resigned the presidency in August 1974, he later blamed Martha Mitchel for Watergate.

Going back to 1970 for a moment, I had the opportunity to fit radio and TV entertainer Jack Benny with hearing aids. I went to Jack's home and was sent up a rather long stairway to his bedroom. I was surprised to find him still in bed. I said his name, he woke-up, got up and got dressed, as I watched. After testing and fitting him, I asked if he would mind me taking a picture receiving a hundred dollars from the comedian who always claimed to be a thirty-nine-year-old miser. He replied, "You'll have to write on it, 'who's paying who!'" A long way from listening to Jack on the radio in 1944.

Jack and Roy who's paying who?

On May 15, 1972, Arthur Bremer shot presidential candidate George Wallace five times at a Maryland rally. And once his diaries were published while he was behind bars, it became clear that he also wanted to assassinate Richard Nixon.

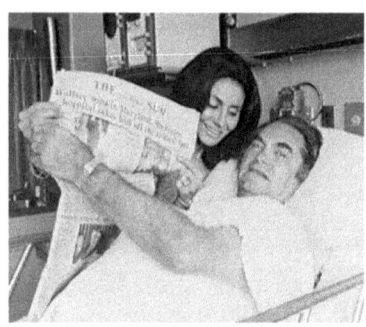

Roy and Bobby

Also in 1973, tennis champions Bobby Rigs and Billie Jean King played each other in what became the "Tennis Battle of the Sexes." Billie Jean walloped Riggs in straight sets. I met Bobby in 1992. In our conversation he described his surgery for prostate cancer which left him without testicles. He told me he wanted to write a book. He said he would call it,

"How to play tennis without any balls!"

"I believe Nixon was a good president but, smart men sometimes do stupid things. The Watergate affair was unnecessary for winning his second term and it brought him down and ruined his legacy!"

CHAPTER ELEVEN

Gerald R. Ford

G erald R. Ford Republican became the thirty-eighth President of the United States when Richard M. Nixon resigned on August 9, 1974.

Gerald Ford is the only American president who was never elected vice president or president by the American people. If you can't trust the choice of Tricky Dick, whose choice can you trust, right? At the time, I, along with many other Americans wondered, "Was he the best for the task or was he selected because he agreed to give Nixon a full pardon?" That pardon came about within one month after Ford took the oath! At best Ford was an "Accidental President!"

On August 20, Ford nominated former New York Governor Nelson Rockefeller to fill the vice presidency he had vacated. Now we had both a president and vice president who had not been elected. Rockefeller was an "Accidental Vice-President!"

Because this book is about the presidents the American people elected during the past one hundred years, I will not spend as much time analyzing the choice of Ford. I will only hit the highlights.

Ford attended the University of Michigan where he played football. He was the MVP as the team won two national championships. He then turned down offers from two NFL teams, the Detroit Lions and the Green Bay Packers.

He modeled for Cosmopolitan magazine in April 1942 with his girlfriend.

He went to Yale Law School until the Japanese bombed Pearl Harbor on December 7, 1941; he enlisted in the U.S. Naval Reserve, serving from 1942 to 1946; he left as a lieutenant commander. Ford then went into politics. During his tenure in Congress, political opponents sometimes referred to Ford's athletic past, including a memorable quote from then President Lyndon B. Johnson that Rep. Ford had, "played too much football without a helmet."

As a Republican congressperson from Michigan, he was undefeated through thirteen elections, so he was a good politician.

Ford was the target of two assassination attempts both in 1975, both in California, and both by women. In Sacramento on September 5, the Secret Service apprehended Lynette "Squeaky" Fromme (a former follower of Charles Manson) after seeing her with a pistol at a crowded event in Capitol Park. Barely two weeks later, radical activist Sara Jane Moore fired a gun at the president in San Francisco, but a fellow bystander (a former Marine) knocked the weapon out of her hand. Both women were sentenced to life in prison; Moore was released on parole in 2009, while Fromme remains in jail.

In 1975, Ford appointed John Paul Stevens as Associate Justice of the Supreme Court of the United States to replace retiring Justice William O. Douglas. After being confirmed, Stevens eventually disappointed some conservatives by siding with the Court's liberal wing regarding the outcome of many key issues. Nevertheless, in 2005 Ford praised Stevens. "He has served his nation well," Ford said of Stevens, "with dignity, intellect and without partisan political concerns."

Ford reluctantly agreed to run for office in 1976, but first he had to counter a challenge by Ronald Reagan. Ford dropped the more liberal Vice President Nelson Rockefeller in favor of US Senator Bob Dole of Kansas.

Bob Dole and Roy

In addition to the pardon dispute and lingering anti-Republican sentiment, Ford had to counter a plethora of negative media imagery.

Televised presidential debates were reintroduced for the first time since the 1960 election. As such, Ford became the first incumbent president to participate in one. Carter later attributed his victory in the election to the debates, saying they "gave the viewers reason to think that Jimmy Carter had something to offer." The turning point came in the second debate when Ford blundered by stating, "There is no Soviet domination of Eastern Europe and there never will be under a Ford Administration." Ford also said that he did not "believe that the Poles consider themselves dominated by the Soviet

Union." In an interview years later, Ford said he had intended to imply that the Soviets would never crush the *spirits* of Eastern Europeans seeking independence. However, the phrasing was so awkward that questioner Max Frankel was visibly incredulous at the response.

In the end, Carter won the election, receiving 50.1 percent of the popular vote and 297 electoral votes compared with 48.0 percent and 240 electoral votes for Ford.

Ford died on December 26, 2006, at his home in Rancho Mirage, California, of a heart attack. At the time of his death, Ford was the longest-lived U.S. president, having lived ninety-three years and 165 days. He died on the 34th anniversary of President Harry S Truman's death.

CHAPTER TWELVE

Looking Back Fifty Years

A great deal has happened in the past fifty-plus years from 1973 to 1923, with nine leaders who led America through good times and bad times. All the good things didn't happen while being led by Republicans and neither did all the bad things. The same can be said about and is true for the Democrats. Seven presidents have been in power during roughly the first forty years of my life.

During this time, I came to understand that America is the greatest country in the world. America fought through the Revolutionary War that secured American independence from Great Britain, which began on April 19, 1775, followed by the

Declaration of Independence on July 4, 1776. There were 6,800 Americans killed in the revolutionary war.

America survived the Civil War from April 12, 1861, to May 9, 1865, which was fought between the Northern Republicans and the Southern Democrats. Lincoln was the Republican Union leader and Jefferson Davis was the Democrat Confederate leader. The Northern Republicans wanted to abolish slavery and the Southern Democrats wanted slavery to continue. Between 620,000 and 750,000 American soldiers died in this war between the states. The Civil War remains the deadliest military conflict in American history.

Americans fought in WWI and lost 116,000 lives to combat and disease.

It is hard to grasp the hardships during the Great Depression. The unemployment rate peaked in 1933, 25.6 percent of American workers, one in four found themselves unemployed.

America was drawn into and fought through and won World War II with its beginning at Pearl Harbor on December 7, 1941. World War II was the deadliest military conflict in history. An estimated total of seventy to eighty-five million people perished, or about 3 percent of the 2.3 billion (est.) people on Earth between 1939 and 1945. America lost 407,000 lives. The Korean Conflict cost the United States 54,000 lives and fighting in Vietnam we lost 58,000.

With a total around 1.5 million American deaths in wars in the two hundred years from 1775 to 1975, the great lesson I have learned is. . .

FREEDOM IS NOT FREE!

We have had leaders during the past fifty years whose sex life seemed more important than doing the job they were trusted to do. Especially Kennedy and Johnson.

There was political corruption and disappointment. Some made big mistakes that cost us money, lives, and elements of our freedom. There were 9 assassination attempts, 2 were successful at the time.

I hope you are enjoying this trip through recent history, and I hope I have not given you a false picture of the details.

Would you say you are a Liberal or a Conservative? Do you believe we should all work and put all our earnings in a pot and divide it equally? Do you believe you must not spend more than you earn? Do you believe it is important to save for retirement years? **Maybe you are like me,** a Liberal on some things and Conservative on others.

"Round and Round, Up and Down, we go!"

The last fifty years are, of course, more recent and you have probably lived and experienced at least part of it. My job becomes more difficult because now I must deal with the readers biases. The reader has many filters in front of his or her computer and so facts that I present may be changed or rearranged by a closed mind. Keep in mind, like a parachute, the mind works better when it is open. Your opinions may have changed because you have added a few years of experience. Winston Churchill said,

> "If you are under thirty and you are not a liberal, you don't have a heart. If you are over thirty and you are not a conservative, you don't have a brain!"

The reason I mention each president's IQ is because while smart people sometimes do stupid things, you don't become the "leader of the free world" if you are stupid.

The next fifty years starts with a very smart peanut farmer from Georgia with an IQ of 153. He was the first American president who was born in a hospital. (Shows you how smart he was.)

CHAPTER THIRTEEN

James Earl "Jimmy" Carter

J ames Earl "Jimmy" Carter was sworn in as the thirty-ninth President of the United States in 1977.

President Carter and Willie Nelson

No question about it, Jimmy was easy to like and a very nice guy. I have always liked the picture of the president with country singer Willie Nelson. Willie is also a very nice guy. Carter said that his son smoked weed on the roof of the White House with Willie.

Willie and Roy   **Johnny and Roy**

I had the opportunity of fitting Willie's good buddy Waylon Jennings with hearing aids. Willie and Waylon along with Kris Kristofferson and Johnny Cash toured the nation as the Highwaymen. They performed six concerts in California, I had back-stage passes and my wife, Jean and I attended all of them. One night after the Highwaymen had finished their show, I was fitting Waylon with a new set of hearing aids. We were at a backstage private area and there was a party going on in the adjoining room. The room that we were in was a small kitchen and there was no door between it and the other room. I told Waylon it was too noisy, and we would have to finish the fitting at a later time. We then joined the party. I was standing with Waylon when Willie came by. Waylon said to

Willie, "You remember my ear doctor, don't you?" Willie said, "Hi Doc!" (Waylon called me his ear doctor even though he knew that I was not a doctor.) Willie then asked if I wanted some of this as he held up a cigar-sized joint. I took the joint and took a very big hit. I had not smoked much weed prior, and I bent over and started to cough, over and over. Jean thought I was going to die, and everyone else got a big laugh.

Jean drove home.

Roy and Waylon   **Roy with Kris**

Jimmy was born on October 1, 1924, at the Wise Sanitarium in Plains, Georgia, a hospital where his mother was employed as a registered nurse. Plains was a town of six hundred people at the time of Jimmy's birth. He then grew up in a town three miles away named Archery. He recalls the best day of his life being during his childhood when at fourteen years old, his house gained electricity. His father was a farmer who employed a lot of poor Black tenant farmers, and in a small town of about two hundred people, the Carters were some of the only White people, while most of the people who lived in

Archery were Black and depended on Jimmy's father for their living.

Jimmy

Jimmy's father was a staunch segregationist. Earl Carter believed in the inferiority of Black people. By contrast, Jimmy's mother, Lillian, openly ignored segregation and visited Black neighbors' homes.

She was the only White person in the stadium of a Dodgers game to cheer when Jackie Robinson hit a home run. Due to the wealth of Carter's family, Lillian was immune from being ostracized by her White peers, despite their intense judgment. Politically, Jimmy took after his mom more than his dad. Like his mother, he was an oddity in his racial attitudes for his time and place. It didn't help that his father was so strict he whipped Jimmy with a peach tree switch until he bled on numerous occasions.

Jimmy attended Plains High School during the time Plains became impoverished by the Great Depression. The family benefited from New Deal farming subsidies. In 1941, after one year at Georgia Southwestern College, he transferred to the Georgia Institute of Technology in Atlanta. He then earned admission to the Naval Academy in 1943. While at the academy, Jimmy met and fell in love with Rosalynn Smith, a friend of his sister Ruth.

When Jimmy, then a fresh-faced US Naval Academy student, first proposed, Rosalynn Smith as she was known then rejected him because of a promise she made at thirteen to her dying father that she'd finish college before marrying.

She kept her promise and they married only after she graduated from Georgia Southwestern College.

Rosalynn

As Rosalynn recounted in her memoir, *First Lady from Plains*, the pair grew up three years and three miles apart.

There were no girls in town who were her age. So, Rosalynn became best friends with Jimmy's younger sister. "I thought he was the most handsome young man I had ever seen," she wrote.

The pair went on their first date in the summer of 1945, after which Jimmy told his mother, "She's the girl I want to marry." They did so the following year. The two married shortly after his graduation in 1946. After graduating with a Bachelor of Science degree he was commissioned as an Ensign.

In 1952, Carter began an association with the navy's fledgling nuclear submarine program. In March 1953, Carter began nuclear power school. He seemed to be headed towards a very distinguished career in the Navy, but after his father's death and being morally and religiously conflicted about being part of an organization that kills people, Carter quit the navy. It was a decision that caused so much marital strife his wife Rosalynn threatened to divorce him.

"God did not intend for me to spend my life working on instruments of destruction to kill people," he said.

For a while, he took on his father's job as a farmer. He didn't inherit much and had to take out huge loans because his father was land rich, but cash poor. As a farmer, however, Jimmy and Rosalynn Carter were incredibly successful as peanut farmers.

In 1962 Carter announced his campaign for the state senate only fifteen days before the election. Rosalynn Carter was very skilled at politics and loved it, much more than Jimmy did. The two ran a very robust campaign. Early counting of the ballots showed Carter trailing his opponent Homer Moore, but this was the result of fraudulent voting orchestrated by Joe Hurst, the chairman of the Democratic Party in Quitman County. Carter challenged the election result, which was confirmed fraudulent in an investigation. Following this, another election was held, in which Carter won.

In the 1970 gubernatorial election, Carter leaned more conservative, positioning himself as a populist, criticizing his opponent for both his wealth and perceived links to the national Democratic party. Carter came ahead of Sanders in the first ballot by 49 percent to 38 percent in September, leading to a runoff election being held. The subsequent campaign was even more bitter. Despite his early support for civil rights, Carter's appeal to racism grew, criticizing Sanders for supporting Martin Luther King Jr.

Carter won the runoff election with 60 percent of the vote and went on to easily win the general election against the Republican Hal Suit, a local news anchor.

Carter was sworn in as the seventy-sixth governor of Georgia on January 12, 1971.

Carter announced his candidacy for President of the United States on December 12, 1974. His name recognition was two percent, and his opponents derisively asked, "Jimmy who?" In response to this, Carter began to emphasize his name and what he stood for, stating "My name is Jimmy Carter, and I'm running for president." This strategy proved successful; by mid-March 1976, Carter was far ahead of the active contenders for the Democratic presidential nomination. Although Carter was initially dismissed as a regional candidate, he still clinched the Democratic nomination.

On July 15, 1976, Carter chose US Senator from Minnesota Walter F. Mondale as his running mate. Carter and Ford faced off in three televised debates. The debates were the first presidential debates since 1960. Carter began the race with a sizable lead over Ford, who narrowed the gap during the campaign, but lost to Carter in a narrow defeat on November 2, 1976.

James Earl Carter became the thirty-ninth president of the United States.

Jimmy Carter takes the oath

Carter was interviewed by Robert Scheer of *Playboy* for the November 1976 issue, which hit the newsstands a couple of weeks before the election. While discussing his religion's view of pride, Carter said, "I've looked on a lot of women with lust. I've committed adultery in my heart many times." This and his admission in another interview that he did not mind if people uttered the word "fuck" led to a media feeding frenzy and critics lamenting the erosion of boundary between politicians and their private intimate lives.

What I remember about the Carter presidency was long gas lines. Seems as though the world ran out of fossil fuel. We discovered fossil fuel was still there, but all the "dip sticks" were in Washington.

Art with Jean and me

In 1978, I decided my hearing aid manufacturing company needed the endorsement of a celebrity so I began to ask everyone who would be the best celebrity for the senior population. Most everyone agreed, television personality **Art Linkletter** was the man we wanted. Now the question, "How could I get him?" Art had two national TV shows, *House Party* in the daytime and *People Are Funny* at night. We didn't have any extra money to offer for his services. I started by calling his agent, Irvin Atkins in Beverly Hills and spoke to him. I told him what I had in mind. He told me they received thirty calls like this every week, but my story was interesting and invited me to come and see him. I explained my idea to Art and Irv, and they seemed to like it. They felt that the senior market who were our customers, was Art's audience. Art then asked me how I expected to pay them, and I said,

> "To be honest with you, sir, I never expected to get this far and hadn't figured it out."

I then told him, "I guess I could give you a part of what we bring in, say ten percent? They looked at each other and smiled and Art held out his hand and said, "You seem to be an honest man so that sounds good to me." We shook hands on it and never ever put anything into writing.

In 1978 I mentioned to Irv Atkins that Roy Rogers was my all-time hero, and he arranged a meeting with **Art Rush**, who was Roy's agent for over forty years. Art Rush set up a meeting for me with Roy Rogers.

What a treat it was to meet my all-time hero, a dream come true. WOW! Jean was with me and said when Roy Rogers walked in it was like sunshine entering the room.

I made an appointment to test Roy's hearing. Roy had a moderate high frequency hearing impairment. Roy did not want to be seen with hearing aids. He said hearing aids did not fit the "King of the Cowboys" image. I fitted Roy with a set of deep canal hearing aids that could not be seen, which made him happy. Over the next few years, Roy Rogers, the King of the Cowboys, my childhood hero, became my very best friend. I shall always treasure the time I spent with him.

Two Roy's

We went to breakfast or lunch in Victorville a couple times every month. Sometimes it was just Roy and me, and often Jean and Dale came along. After four years of friendship, Roy and Dale along with Jean and I were having lunch. Roy leaned over and asked me if I would like him to endorse our hearing aids. Of course, I accepted and asked if I should get in touch with Art Rush. He said that was not necessary that we could do it together. He said he thought he could say,

> *"Ever since I got my Nu-Ear hearing aids,*
> *I hear every word the minister speaks,*
> *every note the choir sings and*
> *Dale doesn't have to holler at me anymore!"*

I then asked him how I should pay him. He put his arm around my shoulder and said, "You are my friend, don't worry about it!" He never charged me a dime. On the way back to the museum, he was driving and looked back at me and said, "You know if you had ever asked me to endorse your products, I had planned to tell you no. It's because you never asked that I decided to do it." Roy gave me a free hand using his likeness and his good name. To think that this great man with his great reputation placed such trust in me was one of the greatest honors I have ever received.

Add Roy Clark for a trio of Roy's

Carter's presidency in the last two years was marked by double-digit inflation, coupled with very high interest rates, oil shortages, and slow economic growth. Both inflation and interest rates rose, economic growth, job creation, and consumer confidence declined sharply. Inflation rose to 7.7 percent in 1978. The sudden doubling of crude oil prices by OPEC, the world's leading oil exporting cartel, forced inflation to double-digit levels, averaging 11.3 percent in 1979 and 13.5 percent in 1980. The sudden shortage of gasoline as the 1979 summer vacation season began, exacerbated the problem, and would come to symbolize the crisis among the public in general; the acute shortage, originating in the shutdown of Amerada Hess refining facilities, led to a lawsuit against the company that year by the federal government.

Sadat   Carter   Menachem

Carter invited the Egyptian president Anwar Sadat and Israeli prime minister Menachem to the presidential lodge at Camp David in September 1978, in hopes of creating a definitive Middle East peace. The negotiations resulted in Egypt formally recognizing Israel, and the creation of an elected government in the West Bank and Gaza. This resulted in the Camp David Accords, which ended the war between Israel and Egypt.

On November 4, a group of Iranian students took over the US Embassy in Tehran. The students belonged to the Muslim Student Followers of the Imam's Line and were in support of the Iranian Revolution. Fifty-two American diplomats and citizens were held hostage for the next 444 days. Carter stated his commitment to resolving the dispute without "any military action that would cause bloodshed or arouse the unstable captors of our hostages to attack them or to punish them." On April 7, 1980, Carter issued Executive Order 12205, imposing economic sanctions against Iran, and announced further measures being taken by members of his cabinet and the American government that he deemed necessary to ensure a safe release.

On April 24, 1980, Carter ordered Operation Eagle Claw to try to free the hostages. The mission failed, leaving eight American servicemen dead and causing the destruction of two aircraft. The ill-fated rescue attempt led to the self-imposed resignation of US Secretary of State Cyrus Vance, who had been opposed to the mission from the beginning.

Communists under the leadership of Nur Muhammad Taraki seized power in Afghanistan on April 27, 1978. The new regime signed a treaty of friendship with the Soviet Union in December of that year. However, due to the regime's efforts to improve secular education and redistribute land being accompanied by mass executions and political oppression, Taraki was deposed by rival Hafizullah Amin in September. Amin was considered a "brutal psychopath" by foreign observers and had lost control of much of the country, prompting the Soviet Union to invade Afghanistan on December 24, 1979, execute Amin, and install Babrak Karmal as president.

The Soviets were unable to quell the insurgency and withdrew from Afghanistan in 1989, precipitating the dissolution of the Soviet Union itself.

Carter's campaign for re-election in 1980 was based primarily on attacking Ronald Reagan. The Carter campaign frequently pointed out and mocked Reagan's proclivity to gaffes, using his age and perceived lack of connection to his native California voter base against him

Carter had to run against his own "stagflation" ridden economy, while the hostage crisis in Iran dominated the news every week. He was attacked by conservatives for failing to "prevent Soviet gains" in less-developed countries, as pro-Soviet governments had taken power in countries including Angola, Ethiopia, Nicaragua, and Afghanistan. His brother, Billy Carter, caused controversy due to his association with Muammar Gaddafi's regime in Libya. He alienated liberal college students, who were expected to be his base, by re-instating registration for the military draft.

On October 28, Carter and Reagan participated in the sole presidential debate of the election cycle. Though initially trailing Carter by several points, Reagan experienced a surge in polling following the debate. This was in part influenced by Reagan deploying the phrase *"There you go again,"* which became the defining phrase of the election. Reagan defeated Carter in a landslide, winning 489 electoral votes. The Senate went Republican for the first time since 1952. In his concession speech,

Carter was viewed as a sincere, honest, and well-meaning southerner. Carter began his term with a 66 percent approval rating, which had dropped to 34 percent approval by the time he left office, with 55 percent disapproving.

In the 1980 presidential campaign, former California Governor Ronald Reagan projected an easy self-confidence, in contrast to Carter's serious and introspective temperament. Carter was portrayed as pessimistic and indecisive in comparison to Reagan, who was known for his charm and delegation of tasks to subordinates. Reagan used the economic problems, Iran hostage crisis, and lack of Washington cooperation to portray Carter as a weak and ineffectual leader.

Carter's presidency was initially viewed by scholars as a failure. However, Carter's post-presidency activities have been favorably received. *The Independent* wrote, "Carter is widely considered a better man than he was a president." Although his presidency received a mixed reception, his peacekeeping and humanitarian efforts since he left office have made Carter renowned as one of the most successful ex-presidents in American history.

Carter attempted to calm various conflicts around the world, most visibly in the Middle East with the signing of the Camp David Accords; giving back the Panama Canal to Panama; and signing the SALT II nuclear arms reduction treaty with Soviet leader Leonid Brezhnev.

His final year was marred by the Iran hostage crisis, which contributed to his losing the 1980 election to Ronald Reagan.

John Hinckley Jr. came close to shooting Carter in March 1981 during his re-election campaign, but he lost his nerve.

When President Jimmy Carter left the White House in 1981, he was fifty-six years old and deep in debt. His peanut business, which sold certified seed peanuts and other farm supplies, was one million in the red by the time he finished his term, the *Washington Post* reports. Carter had been managing the family-owned peanut farm, warehouse and store in Plains, Georgia, since his dad died in 1953, but when he became president, he put it into a blind trust to avoid conflicts of interest. When he left office, "We thought we were going to lose everything." Rosalynn told the Post

We were forced to sell the company, Carter started writing books to generate income. Today, the ninety-four-year-old has published more than thirty, from a children's book to reflections on his presidency.

> **"I considered Jimmy Carter to be a 'Mother Teresa' nice guy. Not strong enough to handle many of the problems of the presidency."**

CHAPTER FOURTEEN

Ronald W. Reagan

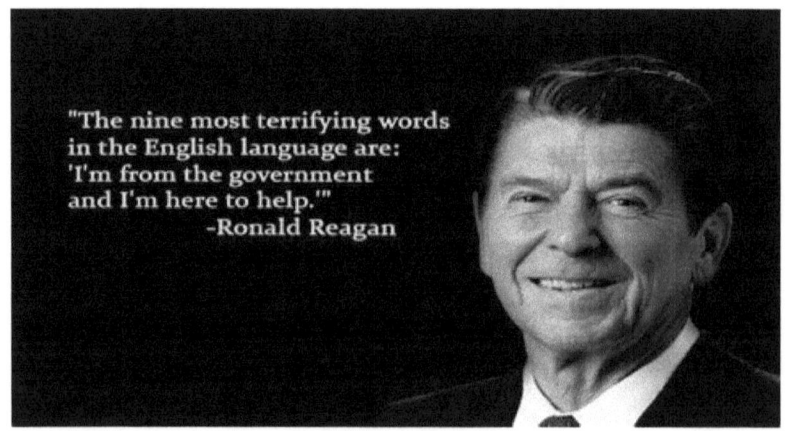

On February 6, 1911, Ronald was born in an apartment on the second floor of a commercial building in Tampico, Illinois to Nelle and John Reagan. Ron's father nicknamed his son "Dutch," due to his "fat little Dutchman" appearance and Dutch-boy haircut; the nickname stuck with him. His father was a shoe salesman, and the family was poor. He attended high school in nearby Dixon and then worked his way through Eureka College. There, he studied economics and sociology, played on the football team, and acted in school plays. He was elected student body president and participated in student protests against the college president. Upon graduation, he became a radio sports announcer. His specialty was creating play-by-play accounts of games using only basic descriptions that the station received by wire as the games were in progress. While traveling with the Cubs in California in 1937, Reagan took a screen test that led to a seven-year contract with Warner Brothers Studios. During the next two decades he appeared in fifty-three films. In 1940 he played the role of George Gipp in the film *Knute Rockne, All American*; from it, he acquired the lifelong nickname "the Gipper."

Dutch

From his first marriage to actress Jane Wyman, he had two children, Maureen and Michael. Maureen passed away in 2001. In 1952, he married Nancy Davis, who was also an actress, and they had two children, Patricia Ann and Ronald Prescott.

Ron, Nancy, and kids

Jane Wyman

As president of the Screen Actors Guild, Reagan became embroiled in disputes over the issue of Communism in the film industry; his political views shifted from liberal to conservative. He toured the country as a television host, becoming a spokesman for conservatism.

In 1955 Reagan, Bob Cunnings, and Art Linkletter opened Disneyland for Walt Disney. In 1962, Reagan changed from Democrat to Republican. He said he didn't leave the Democrat Party, it left him.

Reagan, Cummings and Linkletter

In 1966 Ronald Reagan was elected Governor of California. He was re-elected in 1970. Linkletter always referred to Reagan as "Dutch."

After four years of Jimmy Carter, I felt we needed someone strong with a positive attitude as president. On October 18, 1973, I wrote a letter and donated to Governor Reagan suggesting he run for the presidency of the United States. Governor Reagan returned my check with the following letter.

Ronald Reagan
GOVERNOR

Office of the Governor
STATE CAPITOL
SACRAMENTO 95814

October 18, 1973

Mr. Roy Bain
Beltone Hearing Aid Service
6716 Magnolia Avenue
Riverside, California 92506

Dear Mr. Bain:

I am honored that you mention me in connection with the Presidency. I have however, made no plans for the future beyond 1974, so I am therefore, returning your generous check. I am concerned with making the balance of my term as Governor a period of accomplishment, the tax control initiation having top priority at the moment.

I appreciate your writing and hope that my actions as Governor will continue to warrant your support.

Sincerely,

Ronald Reagan

RONALD REAGAN
Governor

Enclosures

(NOT PRINTED AT GOVERNMENT EXPENSE)

After receiving the Republican nomination, Reagan selected one of his opponents from the primaries, George H. W. Bush, to be his running mate.

The 1980 presidential election featured Reagan against incumbent president Jimmy Carter and was conducted amid a multitude of domestic concerns as well as the ongoing Iran hostage crisis. Reagan's campaign stressed some of his fundamental principles: lower taxes to stimulate the economy, less government interference in people's lives, states' rights, and a strong national defense. Reagan made it clear that, as president he would not allow Iran to hold our Americans hostages for another day.

His relaxed and confident appearance during the televised Reagan/Carter debate on October 28th boosted his popularity and helped to widen his lead in the polls. During the debate Reagan asked,

*"Are you better off today
than you were four years ago?"*

The Reagans' inaugural parade

Ronald Wilson Reagan became the fortieth President of the United States on January 20, 1981. Reagan's IQ was 130.

Ronald Reagan takes the oath of office

Reagan was sixty-nine years, 349 days of age when he was sworn into office for his first term making him the oldest first-term president at the time. *Minutes after Reagan took the oath of office, the United States hostages were released from Iran.*

My wife Jean and I were invited to and attended the Reagan inauguration. We arrived in DC on a Saturday. The next day was the first gala party with the Reagan's in attendance. I was relaxing in the bathtub after the long flight from California when I heard Jean crying. The reason for her sadness was the fact that none of the very expensive beaded formal dresses fit her. I got out of the tub and told her not to worry that I would get them altered. Yeah right, on a Saturday night in a strange town? I got on the phone, lucked out and found a very nice lady who said she could help. We went to her shop in downtown DC. At first, to say the least, we were worried. Her storefront was an elevator door. We got in and went up one floor. When the elevator door opened, we were in her one room shop, which was a mess with pieces of scrap material all over the floor. And yet we could tell by the way she handled the dresses she knew what she was doing. Turned out she did the alterations for Garfinkel's Department Store across the street. She worked through the night and solved the problem. The next evening, we were at an auditorium listening to Pat Boone's daughter Debbie sing, *You Light Up My Life* to Ronald Reagan.

I remember the comedian Rich Little saying, "We've been to the Moon, now Ronald is going to go to the sun. But sir, the sun is hot, and you will burn up." Reagan responded, "I'm going to go at night!"

George and Barbara Bush

On another night we met Vice President George H. W. Bush and Barbara.

Little on Jonny Carson   **Bob Hope**

There were nine major Inaugural Balls. We went to the one at the Kennedy Center along with other people from California. Most of the others there were movie stars, **Bob Hope, Rich Little** and such. The place was so crowded we decided to leave before the Reagans showed up so we could get into a restaurant early. As we were going out of the center, **General Omar Bradley** was being wheeled in, in his wheelchair, I took a great close-up picture. Unfortunately, I had a new camera and none of the pictures came out. When we reached the front of the building, the caravan of limos carrying the Reagan's pulled up. We only caught a glimpse of the President and Nancy. We went to Jean Paul Italian Restaurant. Our table was in the center of this very crowded Italian restaurant and in the middle of the meal everyone seated at the other tables began to sing. Turns out we were in the middle of a portion of the Mormon Tabernacle Choir. They had been listening to the live music presented by a three-piece Italian operatic group and decided to sing for them as a way of saying thank you. Talk about stereo, wow!

General Omar Bradley

On March 30, 1981, President Ronald Reagan was shot and wounded by John Hinckley Jr. in Washington DC as he was returning to his limousine after a speaking engagement at the Washington Hilton. Hinckley believed the attack would impress actress Jodie Foster, with whom he had developed an erotomaniac obsession.

Reagan was seriously wounded by a .22 long rifle bullet that ricocheted off the side of the presidential limousine and hit him in the left underarm, breaking a rib, puncturing a lung, and causing serious internal bleeding. He was close to death upon arrival at George Washington University Hospital but was stabilized in the emergency room, then underwent emergency exploratory surgery. He recovered and was released from the hospital on April 11. No formal invocation of presidential succession took place, though Secretary of State Alexander Haig stated that he was "in control here" while Vice President George H. W. Bush returned to Washington from Fort Worth, Texas.

White House press secretary James Brady, Secret Service agent Tim McCarthy, and DC police officer Thomas Delahanty were also wounded. All three survived, but Brady suffered brain damage and was permanently disabled. His death in 2014 was considered a homicide because it was ultimately caused by his injury.

Hinckley was found not guilty by reason of insanity on charges of attempting to assassinate the president. He remained confined to St. Elizabeth's Hospital, a DC psychiatric facility. In January 2015, federal prosecutors announced that they would not charge Hinckley with Brady's death, despite the medical examiner's classification of his death as a homicide. Hinckley was released from institutional psychiatric care on September 10, 2016. Hinckley was granted his freedom on June 15, 2022. He was considered to "no longer be a danger to himself or others."

In April 1981 Jean and I were invited and went back to the White House.

It was one month after the president had been shot by Hinkley, so the president was a no-show.

The next year when we went to the White House, President Reagan and Nancy were there. After the president gave a short talk, he and Nancy came right over to Jean and me. I asked if it would be appropriate to kiss the first lady, she leaned forward, and I kissed her on the cheek. My friend with the camara didn't take the picture. I did however get a good picture of myself and the President.

The President and me

Nancy and Ron

A few weeks after being at the White House and kissing First Lady Nancy on the cheek, I traveled to Hyannis Port to hold a Success Seminar at Cape Cod. Jean and my two sons had just bought me a new leather carry-on for my birthday. It was black leather and had my name lettered in gold. It was my first bag with wheels. I was very proud of my new bag and would not "check it" when traveling. On the short flight from Boston to Hyannis Port I had to check it. The airline made it known that this DC3 was the oldest active plane in commercial duty. Somehow the airline figured out how to tear a hole in my new carry-on and they lost all my electronic equipment. I was not a happy camper! I had to conduct my seminar without my equipment. When the seminar was over the airline delivered my equipment to me at the hotel. So now I had to cart it all back to the airport and ship it home. The airline clerk told me it would cost me ninety dollars to send it back to San Diego. I was in the middle of a debate with the clerk arguing that, considering they had lost my equipment and I didn't get to use it and on top of that, they tore a hole in my bag, I didn't believe that I should be charged to send it home. I asked the clerk for the name of the president of the airline so I could write him a formal complaint. Suddenly, over my shoulder came an arm moving me to the side. I turned and found myself face-to-face with Senator Ted Kennedy, and he said, "I would also like the name of the president of the airline so I can write and tell him what a jerk this guy is being." I responded, "You have no idea what we are talking about, that's what you always do. I've always thought you were an asshole, and now I know it!" Kennedy stood there and never said another word. After Kennedy checked his young lady friend in for her flight and left, the clerk came over to me and tore up my American Express voucher and said, "I've always thought he was an asshole too, I'm not going to charge you." So, within one month I hugged the President of the United States, kissed the First Lady, and told Senator Ted Kennedy he was an asshole. It was a very good month for the kid who topped garlic in the fields of Gonzales.

Edward Kennedy

On July 7, 1981, Reagan announced that he planned to nominate **Sandra Day O'Connor** as the first woman associate justice of the Supreme Court of the United States, replacing the retiring Justice Potter Stewart. He had pledged during his 1980 presidential campaign that he would appoint the first woman to the Court. On September 21, O'Connor was confirmed by the US Senate with a vote of 99–0.

Reagan and O'Connor

When Reagan took office inflation was at 13 percent. Reagan introduced "supply-side" economics which became known as "Reaganomics" that featured "trickle-down" tax cuts. Reagan never achieved a balanced budget however, the gross domestic product (GDP), which is a monetary measure of the market value of all the final goods and services produced in a specific time period by a country, went from .03 to 4.1 during Reagan's first term and grew during his eight years in office at an annual rate of 7.9 percent per year, with a high of 12.2 percent growth in 1981.

In August 1981, PATCO, the union of federal air traffic controllers, went on strike, violating a federal law prohibiting government unions from striking. Declaring the situation an emergency as described in the 1947 Taft–Hartley Act, Reagan stated that if the air traffic controllers "do not report for work within forty-eight hours, they have forfeited their jobs and will be terminated."

At the time I thought that was a very risky decision. Now when I consider it, it doesn't seem risky at all. When Reagan came into office one of his first moves was to put a picture of Calvin Coolidge on the wall. Turns out that Silent Cal was one of Reagans favorite presidents. Many of Reagans great ideas were first done by Coolidge. Reagan basically copied the Coolidge strategy when he handled the police strike in 1919 when he was the Governor of Massachusetts. It worked well for Calvin in 1919 and it worked well for Reagan sixty-two years later.

The controllers did not return, and on August 5th Reagan fired 11,345 striking air traffic controllers who had ignored his order. Reagan brought in supervisors and military controllers to handle the nation's commercial air traffic until new controllers could be hired and trained. Like the approval of Coolidge's action, the firing of PATCO employees not only demonstrated a clear resolve by the president to take control of the bureaucracy, but it also sent a clear message to the private sector that unions no longer needed to be feared.

His policy of **peace through strength** resulted in a record peacetime defense buildup including a 40 percent real increase in defense spending between 1981 and 1985.

During Reagan's presidency, federal income tax rates were lowered significantly with the signing of the Economic Recovery Tax Act of 1981, which lowered the top marginal tax bracket from 70 percent to 50 percent over three years, and the lowest bracket from 14 percent to 11 percent. One action he made that I didn't care for and still don't was when he separated an earners income into two categories. Before he did that you could write your real-estate losses off your work earnings. Now you are limited when writing passive income (investment income) off your regular income.

Reagan signed legislation establishing a federal
Martin Luther King Jr. holiday!

In a speech to the National Association of Evangelicals on March 8, 1983, Reagan called the Soviet Union "an evil empire."

Reagan's opponent in the 1984 presidential election was former vice president Walter Mondale. Following a weak performance in the first presidential debate, Reagan's ability to win another term was questioned. Reagan rebounded in the second debate; confronting questions about his age, he quipped: "I will not make age an issue of this campaign. I am not going to exploit, for political purposes, my opponent's youth, and inexperience." This remark generated applause and laughter, even from Mondale himself. Reagan won 58.8 percent of the popular vote to Mondale's 40.6 percent. Reagan was sworn in as president for the second time on January 20, 1985, in a private ceremony at the White House. At the time, the seventy-three-year-old Reagan was the oldest person to take the presidential oath of office.

The U S and Saudi Arabia supplied money and arms to the anti-Soviet fighters in Afghanistan in 1985.

They were instrumental in training, equipping and leading Mujahideen against the Soviet Army. President

Reagan's Covert Action program has been given credit for assisting in ending the Soviet occupation of Afghanistan.

Reagan increased defense spending 35 percent but sought to improve relations with the Soviet Union. In dramatic meetings with Soviet leader Mikhail Gorbachev, he negotiated a treaty that would eliminate intermediate-range nuclear missiles. Relations between Libya and the United States under President Reagan were continually contentious, beginning with the Gulf of Sidra incident in 1981. Libyan leader Muammar Gaddafi was considered by the CIA to be, along with USSR leader Leonid Brezhnev and Cuban leader Fidel Castro, part of a group known as the "unholy trinity" and was also labeled as "our international public enemy number one" by a CIA official. These tensions were later revived in early April 1986, when a bomb exploded in a Berlin discothèque, resulting in the injury of sixty-three American military personnel and death of one serviceman. Stating that there was "irrefutable proof" that Libya had directed the "terrorist bombing," Reagan authorized the use of force against the country. In the late evening of April 15, 1986, the United States launched a series of airstrikes on ground targets in Libya.

The attack was designed to halt Gaddafi's "ability to export terrorism," offering him "incentives and reasons to alter his criminal behavior." The president addressed the nation from the Oval Office after the attacks had commenced, stating, "When our citizens are attacked or abused anywhere in the world on the direct orders of hostile regimes, we will respond so long as I'm in this office."

"Mr. Gorbachev, tear down this wall," also known as the Berlin Wall Speech, was a speech delivered by Reagan in West Berlin on June 12, 1987. Reagan called for the General Secretary of the Communist Party of the Soviet Union, Mikhail Gorbachev, to open the Berlin Wall, which had separated West and East Berlin since 1961. The name is derived from a key line in the middle of the speech: "Mr. Gorbachev, tear down this wall!"

Though Reagan's speech received relatively little media coverage at the time, it became widely known after the fall of the Berlin Wall in 1989. In the post-Cold War era, it was often seen as one of the most memorable performances of an American president in Berlin after John F. Kennedy's "Ich bin ein Berliner" speech of 1963.

The Iran–Contra affair became a political scandal in the United States during the 1980s. The scandal stemmed from the use of proceeds from covert arms sales to Iran during the Iran Iraq War to fund the Contra rebels fighting against the government in Nicaragua, funding which had been specifically outlawed by an act of Congress. The International Court of Justice, whose jurisdiction to decide the case was disputed by the United States, ruled that the United States had violated international law and breached treaties in Nicaragua in various ways. Reagan later withdrew the agreement between the United States and the International Court of Justice.

President Reagan professed that he was unaware of the plot's existence. Reagan's popularity declined from 67 percent to 46 percent in less than a week, the most significant and quickest decline ever for a president. The scandal resulted in eleven convictions and fourteen indictments within Reagan's staff.

In his second term, Reagan had three opportunities to fill a Supreme Court vacancy. When Chief Justice Warren Burger retired in September 1986, Reagan nominated incumbent Associate Justice William Rehnquist to succeed Burger as Chief Justice. Then, following Rehnquist's confirmation, the president named Antonin Scalia to fill the vacancy. Reagan's final opportunity to fill a vacancy arose in mid-1987 when Associate Justice Lewis F. Powell Jr. announced his intention to retire. Reagan initially chose conservative jurist Robert Bork to succeed Powell. Bork's nomination was strongly opposed by civil and women's rights groups, and by Senate Democrats. Opposition to his nomination centered on his perceived willingness to roll back the civil rights rulings of the Warren and Burger courts, and his role in the Saturday Night Massacre during the Watergate scandal. Bork's nomination was rejected by a vote of 42–58. Reagan then nominated Douglas Ginsburg to the Court. However, before his name was submitted to the Senate, Ginsburg withdrew himself from consideration. Anthony Kennedy was subsequently nominated and confirmed as Powell's successor.

Early in his presidency, Reagan started wearing custom-made, Starkey In-The-Ear hearing instruments. The instruments were fitted to the President by Byron Burton. Byron was a good friend and mentor of mine. Reagan's decision to go public in 1983 regarding his wearing the hearing instruments influenced a huge number of Americans to have their hearing evaluated and accept the use of amplification.

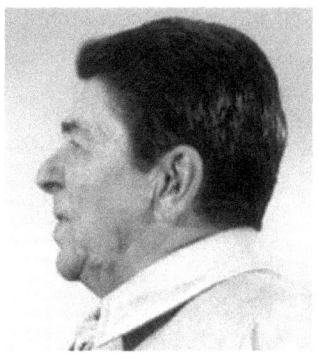

Reagan's Hearing Instruments

A bit about hearing impairment

President Reagan's experience was not exceptional. Within the English language the low frequencies, the vowels, give the words their power, the high frequencies, the consonants, give the words their meaning. Hearing nerve damage due to the aging process affects the least-protected high frequency nerve endings in the cochlea. As a result, a person with high frequency nerve damage will hear low-frequency men's voices better than high-frequency women and children's voices. They will hear some of their male friends very well; they therefore tend to believe some people, especially women and children, just don't speak clearly. We hear with your ears; understanding what we hear takes place in the auditory cortex of our brain. If our ears send only part of the message to our brain, we hear sound loud enough, but we cannot understand the words.

We feed our body through our mouth.

We feed our mind through our senses.

If our senses grow dim, our mind grows dim!

According to recent research conducted at Johns Hopkins University, a loss of hearing is a contributing factor to **Alzheimer's Disease!** Did Reagan's loss of hearing affect his ability to make the right decisions running the country towards the end of his presidency? It's a strong MAYBE!

In August 1994, at the age of eighty-three, former President Reagan was diagnosed with Alzheimer's disease, an incurable neurodegenerative disease which destroys brain cells and ultimately causes death. In November of that year, he informed the nation of the diagnosis through a handwritten letter, writing in part:

"I have recently been told that I am one of the millions of Americans who will be afflicted with Alzheimer's Disease ... At the moment I feel just fine. I intend to live the remainder of the years God gives me on this earth doing the things I have always done. I now begin the journey that will lead me into the sunset of my life. I know that for America there will always be a bright dawn ahead. Thank you, my friends. May God always bless you."

After his diagnosis, letters of support from well-wishers poured into his California home. However, there was also speculation over how long Reagan had demonstrated symptoms of mental degeneration. In a 2011 book titled *My Father at 100*, Reagan's son Ron said he had suspected early signs of his father's dementia as early as 1984; an allegation that sparked a furious response from his brother, Michael, who accused him of, selling out his father to sell books. In her book *Reporting Live*, former CBS White House correspondent Lesley Stahl recounted that in her final meeting with the president in 1986, Reagan did not seem to know who she was. Stahl wrote that she came close to reporting that Reagan was senile, but by the end of the meeting, he had regained his alertness.

Neurosurgeon Daniel Ruge, who served as Physician to the President from 1981 to 1985, said that he never detected signs of the disease while speaking almost every day with Reagan. John E. Hutton, who served from 1985 to 1989, said the president "absolutely" did not "show any signs of dementia or Alzheimer's."

Reagan died of pneumonia, complicated by Alzheimer's disease, at his home in the Bel Air district of Los Angeles, California, on the afternoon of **June 5, 2004**. A short time after his death, Nancy Reagan released a statement saying, "My family and I would like the world to know that President Ronald Reagan has died after ten years of Alzheimer's disease at ninety-three years of age. We appreciate everyone's prayers." Speaking in Paris, France, President George W. Bush called Reagan's death "a sad hour in the life of America." He also declared June 11 a National Day of Mourning.

A few Reagan quotes:

> "Freedom is a fragile thing and is never more than one generation away from extinction. It is not ours by inheritance; it must be fought for and defended constantly by each generation, for it comes only once to a people. Those who have known freedom, and then lost it, have never known it again."

> "A recession is when a neighbor loses his job. A depression is when you lose yours."

> "Republicans believe every day is the Fourth of July, but the democrats believe every day is April 15."

"You know, it has been said that politics is the second oldest profession and I've come to realize over the last few years, it bears a great similarity to the first."

"Government is not the solution to our problem; government is the problem."

"Government is like a baby. An alimentary canal with a big appetite at one end and no sense of responsibility at the other."

"Ronald Reagan was the first president whom I knew personally. He was extremely sharp, and I though he was a great president!"

CHAPTER FIFTEEN

George H.W. Bush

On September 2, 1944, in the treacherous waters near Chichi Jima, the site of a Japanese military base on one of the Bonin Islands, approximately 150 miles north of Iwo Jima, an American airman who had been shot down was fished out of the Pacific Ocean by the rescue submarine, Finback. That airman was **George H.W. Bush**.

George Herbert Walker Bush was a war hero. And he was a war hero because of his love, honor, and duty to his country.

Just don't ask George Bush if he was a war hero.

"It was just part of my duty. People say, 'War Hero'. **How come a guy who gets his airplane shot down is a hero and a guy who's good enough that he doesn't get shot down is not?** Ask John F. Kennedy about it, why are you a hero? They sank my boat. Why am I a hero? They shot down my airplane."

George Herbert Walker Bush was sworn in as the forty-first President of the United States on January 20, 1989.

George H W. Bush becomes President

George was born in Milton, MA. on June 12, 1924. He was the second son of Prescott Bush and Dorothy (Walker) Bush.

George grew up in a very wealthy family.

He attended Greenwich Country Day School and Phillips Academy, an elite private academy in Massachusetts. While at Phillips Academy, he served as president of the senior class and was captain of the varsity baseball and soccer teams.

After graduating from Phillips Academy at eighteen, he enlisted in the United States Navy. He was commissioned as an Ensign in the Naval Reserve at Naval Air Station Corpus Christi on June 9, 1943, becoming one of the youngest aviators in the Navy. Beginning in 1944, Bush served in the Pacific theater, where he flew a Grumman TBF Avenger, a torpedo bomber capable of taking off from aircraft carriers.

George Bush

During an attack on a Japanese installation in Chichi Jima, Bush's aircraft successfully attacked several targets but was downed by enemy fire. Bush successfully bailed out from the aircraft and was rescued by the USS *Finback*. He was later awarded the Distinguished Flying Cross for his role in the mission.

By the end of his period of active service, Bush had flown fifty-eight missions, completed 128 carrier landings, and recorded 1228 hours of flight time.

Bush met Barbara Pierce at a Christmas dance in Greenwich in December 1941, and they married in Rye, New York, on January 6, 1945. They had six children: George W., Robin, Jeb , Neil , Marvin, and Doro. Their oldest daughter, Robin, unfortunately died of leukemia in 1953.

George and Barbara

Bush enrolled at Yale College, where he was the captain of the Yale baseball team and played in the first two College World Series as a left-handed first baseman. He graduated Phi Beta Kappa in 1948 with a Bachelor of Arts degree in economics. He had an IQ of 130. With support from family and friends, Bush and John Overbey launched the Bush-Overbey Oil Development Company in 1951. In 1953 he co-founded the

Zapata Petroleum Corporation, an oil company that drilled in the Permian Basin in Texas. Bush remained involved with Zapata until the mid-1960s, when he sold his stock in the company for approximately one million dollars.

The Bush's in China

President Richard Nixon appointed Bush to the position of Ambassador to the United Nations in 1971 and to the position of chairman of the Republican National Committee in 1973. In 1974 President Gerald Ford appointed him as the Chief of the Liaison Office to the People's Republic of China, and in 1976 Bush became the Director of Central Intelligence. Bush ran for president in 1980 but was defeated in the Republican presidential primaries by Ronald Reagan, who then selected Bush as his vice-presidential running mate.

In the 1988 presidential election, Bush defeated Democrat Michael Dukakis, becoming the first incumbent vice president to be elected president since Martin Van Buren in 1836.

The United States Invasion of Panama, codenamed Operation "Just Cause," lasted over a month between mid-December 1989 and late January 1990. It occurred ten years after the Torrijos–Carter Treaties were ratified to transfer control of the Panama Canal from the United States to Panama by January 1, 2000. The primary purpose of the invasion was to depose the *de facto* Panamanian leader, General Manuel Noriega. He was wanted by the United States for racketeering and drug trafficking. Following the operation, the Panama Defense Forces were dissolved and President-elect Guillermo Endara was sworn into office. The United Nations General Assembly and the Organization of American States condemned the invasion as a violation of international law.

Noriega

Bush presided over the Gulf War, ending the Iraqi occupation of Kuwait in the latter conflict. Though the agreement was not ratified until after he left office, Bush negotiated and signed the North American Free Trade Agreement (NAFTA), which created a trade bloc consisting of the United States, Canada, and Mexico. Bush appointed David Souter and Clarence Thomas to the Supreme Court. Domestically, Bush reneged on a 1988 campaign promise by enacting legislation to raise taxes with the justification of reducing the budget deficit. He also championed and signed three pieces of bipartisan legislation, the Americans with Disabilities Act of 1990, Immigration Act of 1990, and the Clean Air Act Amendments of 1990.

George H.W. Bush rang in the New Year of 1992 with a twelve-day trade-focused trip to Asia and the Pacific to discuss America's post-Cold War readjustment of economic relations and policies. On 8 January 1992, Bush played a doubles tennis match with US ambassador to Japan Michael Armacost against Emperor of Japan Akihito and his son, Crown Prince Naruhito. The emperor and crown prince won. That evening, Bush attended a state event for 135 diplomats held at the Japanese Prime Minister's residence. In between the second and third courses, Bush, who had been scheduled to give remarks at the dinner, fainted in his chair while vomiting in Miyazawa's lap. First Lady Barbara Bush held a napkin to her husband's mouth until the United States Secret Service took over. While still on the floor, Bush quipped to his personal physician, Burton Lee, "Roll me under the table until the dinner's over." He assured dinner guests he had "influenza" and left for the evening. Barbara Bush later gave a speech in President Bush's place where she affectionately teased Armacost for the tennis game and jokingly claimed that defeat was something to which her family was not accustom.

Bush lost the 1992 presidential election to Democrat Bill Clinton following an economic recession, his turnaround on his tax promise, and the decreased emphasis of foreign policy in a post-Cold War political climate. Historians generally rank Bush as an above-average president. After a long battle with vascular Parkinson's disease, Bush died at his home in Houston on November 30, 2018, at the age of ninety-four. At the time of his death he was the longest-lived U.S. president, a distinction now held by Jimmy Carter.

"George was an easy-going president and Barbara was a sweetheart!"

CHAPTER SIXTEEN

William Jefferson Clinton

W illiam Jefferson Clinton served as the forty-second President of the United States from 1993 to 2001.

Vice President Al Gore and President Bill Clinton

Clinton previously served as governor of Arkansas from 1979 to 1981 and again from 1983 to 1992, and as attorney general of Arkansas from 1977 to 1979. A member of the Democratic Party, Clinton became known as a New Democrat, as many of his policies reflected a "centrist Third Way" political philosophy.

Billy Clinton

Bill was born William Jefferson Blythe III on August 19, 1946, at Julia Chester Hospital in Hope, Arkansas. He is the son of William Jefferson Blythe Jr., a traveling salesman who had died in an automobile accident three months before his birth, and Virginia Dell Cassidy. His parents had married on September 4, 1943. Later it was proven to be bigamous, as Blythe was still married to his third wife. Bill's mother, Virginia went to New Orleans to study nursing soon after Bill was born. She left Bill with her parents, who owned and ran a small grocery store. Virginia returned from nursing school and married Roger Clinton Sr., when Bill was four years old. Roger co-owned an automobile dealership in Hot Springs, Arkansas. The family moved to Hot Springs in 1950.

Although he immediately assumed use of his stepfather's surname, it was not until Bill turned fifteen that he formally adopted the surname, Clinton. Bill has described his stepfather as a gambler and an alcoholic who regularly abused his mother and half-brother, Roger.

In Hot Springs, Bill attended St. John's Catholic Elementary School, Ramble Elementary School, and Hot Springs High School, where he was an active student leader, avid reader, and musician. Clinton was in the chorus and played the tenor saxophone, winning first chair in the state band's saxophone section. He briefly considered dedicating his life to music, but as he noted in his autobiography *My Life*, "Sometime in my sixteenth year, I decided I wanted to be in public life as an elected official. I loved music and thought I could be very good, but I knew I would never be John Coltrane or Stan Getz. I was interested in medicine and thought I could be a fine doctor, but I knew I would never be Michael DeBakey. But I knew I could be great in public service."

Bill with President Kennedy

Clinton has identified two influential moments in his life, both occurring in 1963, that contributed to his decision to become a public figure. One was his visit as a Boys Nation senator to the White House to meet President John F. Kennedy. The other was watching Martin Luther King Jr.'s 1963 "I Have a Dream" speech on TV, which impressed him so much that he later memorized it.

Clinton was raised in Arkansas and attended Georgetown University. Clinton's IQ is 156 and he received a Rhodes Scholarship. He later graduated from Yale Law School.

He met Hillary Rodham at Yale; they married in 1975.

Hillary Clinton

Bill ran for the office of Arkansas Attorney General in 1976.

After serving as attorney general, Clinton ran for governor of Arkansas in 1978. He won the Democratic primary comfortably, receiving over 55 percent of the popular vote. Witnessing his strong support during the primaries, Republicans did not nominate a candidate to run against him. Clinton won the general election unopposed. His experience as the attorney general was considered a natural "stepping-stone" to the governorship. Clinton was elected the fortieth and forty-second governor of Arkansas (1979–1981; 1983–1992).

At age thirty-two, he became the nation's youngest governor in January 1979. He lost re-election to the Republican nominee Frank D. White in 1980. After leaving office in January 1981, Clinton self-deprecatingly referred to himself as "the youngest former governor in the history of the country." In 1982 he ran again in the gubernatorial election, defeating Governor White. He contested and won the 1984, 1986, and 1990 gubernatorial elections.

The Persian **Gulf War**, which was triggered by Iraq's invasion of Kuwait began on August 2, 1990. President George H. W. Bush's approval ratings were around 80 percent during the Gulf War, and he was described as unbeatable for re-election. When Bush compromised with Democrats to try to lower federal deficits, he reneged on his promise not to raise taxes, which hurt his approval rating. Bush had stated, "Read my lips; No new taxes!"

Gennifer Flowers

In Clinton's first presidential primary contest, the Iowa Caucus, Clinton finished third to Iowa senator Tom Harkin. During the campaign for the New Hampshire primary, reports surfaced that Clinton had engaged in an extramarital affair with **Gennifer Flowers**. Clinton fell far behind former Massachusetts senator Paul Tsongas in the New Hampshire polls. Following Super Bowl XXVI, Bill and his wife Hillary went on *60 Minutes* to rebuff the charges. Their television appearance was a calculated risk, but Clinton regained several delegates. He finished second to Tsongas in the New Hampshire primary, but after trailing badly in the polls and coming within single digits of winning, the media viewed it as a victory. News outlets labeled him **The Comeback Kid** for earning a firm second-place finish.

Gov. Jerry with Roy & Jerry's father Gov. Pat and my wife, Jean

Winning Florida and Texas and many of the Southern primaries on Super Tuesday gave Clinton a sizable delegate lead. However, former California governor Jerry Brown was scoring victories and Clinton had yet to win a significant contest outside his native South. With no major Southern state remaining, Clinton targeted New York, which had many delegates. He scored a resounding victory in New York City, shedding his image as a regional candidate. Having been transformed into the consensus candidate, he secured the Democratic Party nomination, finishing with a victory in Jerry Brown's home state of California.

Clinton repeatedly condemned Bush for making a promise he failed to keep, not to raise taxes. By election time, the economy was souring, and Bush saw his approval rating plummet to just slightly over 40 percent. Many Democrats who had supported Ronald Reagan and Bush in previous elections switched their support to Clinton.

Clinton won the 1992 presidential election against Republican incumbent George H. W. Bush.

Clinton was inaugurated as the forty-second president of the United States on January 20, 1993, with Al Gore as his vice president.

President Clinton's attorney general Janet Reno authorized the FBI's use of armored vehicles to deploy tear gas into the buildings of the Branch Davidian community near Waco, Texas, in hopes of ending a 51 day siege. During the operation on April 1 9, 1993, the buildings caught fire and seventy-five of the residents died, including twenty-four children. The raid had originally been planned by the Bush administration; Clinton had played no role.

On May 19, 1993, Clinton fired seven employees of the White House Travel Office. This caused the White House travel office controversy even though the travel office staff served at the pleasure of the president and could be dismissed without cause. The White House responded to the controversy by claiming that the firings were done in response to financial improprieties that had been revealed by a brief FBI investigation.

The Battle of Mogadishu occurred in Somalia in 1993. During the operation, two US helicopters were shot down by rocket-propelled grenade attacks to their tail rotors, trapping soldiers behind enemy lines. This resulted in an urban battle that killed eighteen American soldiers, wounded seventy-three others, and one was taken prisoner. There were many more Somali casualties. Some of the American bodies were dragged through the streets—a spectacle broadcast on television news programs. In response, US forces were withdrawn from Somalia and later conflicts were approached with fewer soldiers on the ground.

Clinton appointed two justices to the Supreme Court: Ruth Bader Ginsburg in 1993 and Stephen Breyer in 1994. Both justices went on to serve until the 2020s, leaving a lasting judicial legacy for President Clinton.

In November 1993, David Hale, the source of criminal allegations against Bill Clinton in the Whitewater controversy, alleged that while governor of Arkansas, Clinton pressured Hale to provide an illegal three-hundred-thousand-dollar loan to Susan McDougal, the Clintons' partner in the Whitewater land deal. The Clintons themselves were never charged, and Clinton maintains his and his wife's innocence in the affair.

Paula Jones

In December of the same year, allegations by Arkansas state troopers Larry Patterson and Roger Perry were first reported by David Brock in *The American Spectator*. In the affair later known as "Trooper-gate," the officers alleged that they had arranged sexual liaisons for Clinton back when he was governor of Arkansas. The story mentioned a woman named *Paula*, a reference to **Paula Jones**. Brock later apologized to Clinton, saying the article was politically motivated "bad journalism," and that "the troopers were greedy and had slimy motives."

That month, Clinton implemented a Department of Defense directive known as **Don't Ask, Don't Tell,** which allowed gay men and women to serve in the armed services provided they kept their sexual preferences a secret.

On January 1, 1994, Clinton signed the North American Free Trade Agreement into law. (NAFTA)

January 21, 1994: Ronald Gene Barbour, a retired military officer and freelance writer, plotted to kill Clinton while the president was jogging. Barbour returned to Florida a week later without having fired the shots at the president, who was on a state visit to Russia. Barbour was sentenced to five years in prison and was released in 1998.

November 1994: Osama bin Laden recruited Ramzi Yousef, the mastermind of the 1993 World Trade Center bombing, to attempt to assassinate Clinton. However, Yousef decided that security would be too effective and decided to target Pope John Paul II instead.

In 1996, during his visit to the Asia-Pacific Economic Cooperation (APEC) forum in Manila, Clinton's motorcade was rerouted before it was to drive over a bridge. An intelligence team later discovered a bomb under the bridge. Subsequent US investigation "revealed that the plot was masterminded by a Saudi terrorist living in Afghanistan named Osama bin Laden."

In 1996 it was found that several Chinese foreigners made contributions to Clinton's re-election campaign and the Democratic National Committee with the backing of the People's Republic of China. Some of them also attempted to donate to Clinton's defense fund. This violated United States law forbidding non-American citizens from making campaign contributions.

In October 1997, Clinton announced he was getting hearing aids, due to hearing loss attributed to his age, and his time spent as a musician in his youth.

In February 1997, it was discovered upon documents being released by the Clinton Administration that 938 people had stayed at the White House, and that 821 of them had made donations to the Democratic Party and got the opportunity to stay in the Lincoln bedroom as a result of the donations. Some donors included Steven Spielberg, Tom Hanks, and Jane Fonda. Top donors also got golf games and morning jogs with Clinton as a result of the contributions.

Several women have publicly accused Bill Clinton of sexual misconduct, including rape, harassment, and sexual assault.

Additionally, some commentators have characterized Clinton's sexual relationship with former White House intern Monica Lewinsky as predatory or non-consensual, despite the fact that Lewinsky called the relationship consensual at the time. These allegations have been revisited and lent more credence in 2018, in light of the #MeToo movement, with many commentators and Democratic leaders now saying Clinton should have been compelled to resign after the Lewinsky affair.

In 1994 Paula Jones initiated a sexual harassment lawsuit against Clinton, claiming he had made unwanted advances towards her in 1991; Clinton denied the allegations. Jones the ruling, and her suit gained traction following Clinton's admission to having an affair with Monica Lewinsky in August 1998. In 1998, lawyers for Paula Jones released court documents that alleged a pattern of sexual harassment by Clinton when he was governor of Arkansas. Clinton later agreed to an out-of-court settlement and paid Jones $850,000.

Clinton's second term would be dominated by the **Monica Lewinsky** scandal which began in 1996, when he began a sexual affair with twenty-two-year-old White House intern Monica Lewinsky. In January 1998, news of the sexual relationship made tabloid headlines. The scandal escalated throughout the year, culminating on December 19 when Clinton was impeached by the House of Representatives, becoming the second US president to be impeached after Andrew Johnson. The two impeachment articles that the House passed were centered around Clinton using the powers of the presidency to obstruct the investigation and that he lied under oath. In 1999 Clinton's impeachment trial began in the

Senate, and Clinton was acquitted on both charges as the Senate failed to cast sixty-seven votes against him, the conviction threshold.

Clinton and Monica

In 1998 Kathleen Willey alleged that Clinton had groped her in a hallway in 1993. An independent counsel determined Willey gave "false information" to the FBI, inconsistent with sworn testimony related to the Jones allegation. On March 19, 1998, Julie Hiatt Steele, a friend of Willey, released an affidavit, accusing the former White House aide of asking her to lie to corroborate Ms. Willey's account of being sexually groped by Clinton in the Oval Office. An attempt by Kenneth Starr to prosecute Steele for making false statements and obstructing justice ended in a mistrial, and Starr declined to seek a retrial after Steele sought an investigation against the former Independent Counsel for prosecutorial misconduct. Linda Tripp's grand jury testimony also differed from Willey's claims regarding inappropriate sexual advances.

Kathleen Willey

Also in 1998, Juanita Broadrick alleged that Clinton had raped her in the spring of 1978, although she said she did not remember the exact date. To support her charge, Broadrick notes that she told multiple witnesses in 1978 she had been raped by Clinton, something these witnesses also state in interviews to the press. Broadrick had earlier filed an affidavit denying any "unwelcome sexual advances" and later repeated the denial in a sworn deposition. In a 1998 NBC interview wherein she detailed the alleged rape, Broadrick said she had denied (under oath) being raped only to avoid testifying about the ordeal publicly.

Juanita Broadrick

The Lewinsky scandal has had an enduring impact on Clinton's legacy, beyond his impeachment in 1998. In 2018 Clinton was asked in several interviews about whether he should have resigned, and he said he had made the right decision in not resigning. During the 2018 Congressional elections, the *New York Times* alleged that having no Democratic candidate for office asking Clinton to campaign with them was a change that attributed to the revised understanding of the Lewinsky scandal. Clinton admitted to having extramarital affairs with singer Gennifer Flowers and Monica Lewinsky. Miss America, 1982 Elizabeth Gracen, Miss Arkansas winner Sally Perdue, and Dolly Kyle Browning all claimed that they had affairs with Clinton during his time as governor of Arkansas.

Elizabeth Gracen   **Sally Perdue**

Browning would later sue Clinton, Bruce Lindsey, Robert S. Bennett, and Jane Mayer, alleging they engaged in a conspiracy to attempt to block her from publishing a book loosely based on her relationship with Clinton and tried to defame him. However, Browning's lawsuit was dismissed.

Dolly Browning

On **January 19, 2001,** Clinton's law license was suspended for five years after he acknowledged to an Arkansas circuit court that he had engaged in conduct prejudicial to the administration of justice in the *Jones* case.

Clinton issued 141 pardons and thirty-six commutations on his last day in office on January 20, 2001. Controversy surrounded Marc Rich and allegations that Hillary Clinton's brother, Hugh Rodham, accepted payments in return for influencing the president's decision-making regarding the pardons.

Clinton left office in 2001 with the highest end-of-term approval rating of any US president since Franklin D. Roosevelt. His presidency has been ranked among the upper tier in historical rankings of US presidents. However, his personal conduct and allegations of sexual assault against him have made him the subject of substantial scrutiny.

The Clinton's left the White House sixteen million in debt, he told NBC's Craig Melvin in 2018. As Hillary put it, the couple came out of the White House "dead broke." They were able to climb out of the multi-million-dollar hole via paid speeches and lucrative book deals. In his first year out of office, Bill gave fifty-seven speeches and earned $13.7 million from his speaking and writing business according to their tax return. A single speech generated anywhere from $125,000, the standard fee, to $350,000, NPR reported. By 2004, just three years after leaving office, the Clintons had fully erased their debt. And by the time Hillary ran for president in 2016, her net worth was approximately forty-five million dollars, Forbes estimated. Today, the couple's impressive real estate portfolio includes a $1.7 million home in Chappaqua, New York, and a $2.85 million home in Washington, DC.

"I thought Clinton was a great president, but he was a serial womanizer and as a result, it almost got him impeached."

CHAPTER SEVENTEEN

George Walker Bush

George Walker Bush, served as the forty-third president of the United States from 2001 to 2009.

Bush comes in as Clinton goes out

Bush previously served as the forty-sixth Governor of Texas from 1995 to 2000.

George

Bush attended high school at Phillips Academy, a boarding school in Andover, Massachusetts, where he played baseball and was the head cheerleader during his senior year. He attended Yale University from 1964 to 1968, graduating with a Bachelor of Arts degree in history. He characterized himself as an average student.

In the fall of 1973, Bush entered Harvard Business School. He graduated in 1975 with an MBA degree. *He is the only US president to have earned an MBA.* Bush's IQ of 125 was one of the lowest three of all presidents up until that time.

While Bush was at a backyard barbecue in 1977, friends introduced him to Laura Welch, a schoolteacher and librarian. After a three-month courtship, she accepted his marriage proposal and they wed on November 5th of that year. On November 25, 1981, Laura Bush gave birth to fraternal twin daughters, Barbara and Jenna.

Prior to getting married, Bush struggled with multiple episodes of alcohol abuse.

Laura Bush

In May 1968, Bush was commissioned into the Texas Air National Guard. He was honorably discharged from the Air Force Reserve on November 21, 1974.

Bush remains the most recent president to serve in the military. Of the forty-six US presidents, thirty-one served in uniform.

In 1984 his small oil exploration company merged with the larger Spectrum 7, and Bush became chairman. The company was hurt by decreased oil prices, and it folded into HKN, Inc., with Bush becoming a member of HKN's board of directors.

In April 1989, Bush brought together a group of investors to purchase a controlling interest in the Texas Rangers baseball franchise for eighty-nine million, in which he invested five hundred thousand. He then was managing general partner for five years. He actively led the team's projects and regularly attended its games, often choosing to sit in the open stands with fans. Bush's sale of his shares in the Rangers in 1998 brought him over fifteen million from his initial five hundred thousand investment.

Bush declared his candidacy for the 1994 Texas gubernatorial election at the same time his brother Jeb sought the governorship in Florida. His campaign focused on four themes: welfare reform, tort reform, crime reduction, and education improvement.

After easily winning the Republican primary, Bush faced popular Democratic incumbent Governor Ann Richards. In the course of the campaign, Bush pledged to sign a bill allowing Texans to obtain permits to carry concealed weapons. Richards had vetoed the bill, but Bush signed it into law after he became governor.

Bush used a budget surplus to push through Texas's largest tax-cut, two billion.

In 1999 Bush signed a law that required electric retailers to buy a certain amount of energy from renewable sources (RPS), which helped Texas eventually become the leading producer of wind powered electricity in the US.

In 1998 Bush won re-election with a record 69 percent of the vote. He became the first governor in Texas history to be elected to two consecutive four-year terms.

On July 25, 2000, Bush selected Dick Cheney to be his running mate as he ran for the presidency.

When the election returns were tallied on November 7, 2000, Bush had won twenty-nine states, including Florida. The closeness of the Florida outcome led to a recount. Under Florida election law, a machine recount of all votes cast was required because the margin of victory was less than 0.5 percent. In this race, the gap appeared to be roughly 0.01 percent.

This was a very interesting election. When I turned on any news station, someone was saying, "He's trying to steal the election!" It took a minute to figure out who was calling who a thief. Both Republicans and Democrats claimed the same thing. It was a good example of how justice is determined by the bias of who's making the decision.

Bush v. Gore???

The initial recount also went to Bush, but the outcome was tied up in lower courts for a month. County officials tried to discern voter intent through a cloud of "hanging chads" (incompletely punched paper ballots) and "pregnant chads" (paper ballots that were dimpled, but not pierced, during the voting process), as well as "overvotes" (ballots that recorded multiple votes for the same office) and "undervotes" (ballots that recorded no vote for a given office).

As the case was appealed and moved to a higher court, the presidency went back and forth from Bush to Gore, back to Bush and ended in the Supreme Court. On December 9, in the controversial *Bush v. Gore* ruling, the Court reversed a Florida Supreme Court decision that had ordered a third count, and stopped an ordered statewide hand recount based on the argument that the use of different standards among Florida's counties violated the Equal Protection Clause of the Fourteenth Amendment. In a 5-4 decision Bush won and became the forty-third president.

Gore officially conceded on December 13 and stated in a televised address, "While I strongly disagree with the Court's decision, I accept it."

Bush became the fourth person to be elected president without winning the popular vote, and the only person to win because of a court decision.

Bush taking the Oath

About, eight months into Bush's first term the **September 11 attacks**, commonly referred to as **9/11**, occurred. Four commercial airliners traveling from the northeastern US to California were hijacked mid-flight by nineteen-al-Qaeda terrorists. Their explicit goal was to crash each plane into a prominent American building. The first plane to hit its target was American Airlines Flight 11. It was crashed into the North Tower of the World Trade Center complex in Lower Manhattan at 8:46 am. Seventeen minutes later at 9:03 am, the World Trade Center's South Tower was hit by United Airlines Flight 175. Both 110-story towers collapsed within an hour and forty-two minutes, leading to the collapse of the other World Trade Center structures including 7 World Trade Center, and significantly damaging surrounding buildings. A third hijacked flight, American Airlines Flight 77, crashed into the west side of the Pentagon (the headquarters of the American military) in Arlington County, Virginia at 9:37 am, causing a partial collapse of the building's side.

The fourth, and final, flight United Airlines Flight 93, was flown in the direction of Washington, DC. The plane's passengers were alerted about the previous attacks and attempted to regain control of the aircraft away from the hijackers and prevent the aircraft from crashing into its intended target. A struggle broke out in the aircraft and the hijackers crashed the plane in a field near Shanksville, Pennsylvania, at 10:03 a.m. Investigators determined that Flight 93's target was either the US Capitol or the White House.

On September 11, 2001, Jean and I started watching TV in amazement as the second plane hit the second World Trade Center tower. And shortly thereafter both towers came crashing down. Never in our lifetime had anything like this happened, we thought we were at war. Like most Americans we became very patriotic. I went to the flag store to buy a flag. They said they only had one flag left and it was big. I handed them my credit card and said, "I'll take it!" It cost $1300. I left wondering what I had bought. The box filled the whole back seat of my car. My son Ron and I unpacked it. It was thirty feet high by fifty feet wide. We decided the only place I could display it was by hanging it off the roof of my house. Ron and I got on the roof and unfolded the flag. We then tied the ends of the flag on the roof and draped it down. It covered the whole front of the house. We anchored the bottom on one end with a five-foot post and let the other end blow in the wind. It looked fantastic. Because our house overlooks three major freeways, thousands of people drove by and saw the flag. One of my friends called and jokingly said, "I see American termite company has tented your house!" The first night I was in our spa between the house and the flag. It seemed like I was in a little boat with the American flag as a huge sail.

I was inspired to write a poem. A few days later, a reporter from San Diego Channel 10 News came by and interviewed me. He wanted to hear my story about the flag. During the interview I recited the poem I had just written. The story was on prime-time TV news that evening. A week or so later I received two T-shirts from New York. A group had put my poem on T-shirts and sold them to raise money for the families of 9/11 victims.

I was proud that my poem was used for this purpose. Here is my poem entitled "We the People!"

"We the People"

We the people of America, stand for Liberty.
Brothers and Sisters united, living in the land of the free.
We abide by the Golden Rule; we treat our neighbors' right.
But if our Freedom is threatened, together we shall fight.
Because... We the people of America, stand proud and tall.
And when it comes to one another, it is Liberty for all.

We the people of America, share Equality.
All races and religions, different as can be.
Our nation has grown to greatness, as a melting pot.
A home for every color and proud of all we've got.
For... We the people of America, our future is divine.
These words spoken by our Hero's shall stand the test of time.

"*I know not what course others may take, but as for me . . .
Give me liberty or give me death.*"
"Four score and seven years ago our forefathers brought forth on this continent a new nation, conceived in liberty and dedicated to the proposition that, all men are created equal."
"*Ask not what your country can do for you . . . but what you can do for your country.*"
"I've been to the mountain; I've seen the other side,
And . . . I have a dream."
"*Terrorists attacks can shake the foundation of our biggest buildings, but . . . They cannot touch the foundation of AMERICA.*"

We the people of America, enjoy Prosperity,
We work hard on the farm, and in the factory.
From the mountains to the oceans, across the wide prairie,
Our America is beautiful, from sea to shining sea . . . Yes,

We the people of America, in GOD we trust.
GOD bless America, and every one of US.
Roy Bain ©2004 rewrite

The terrorist attacks on 9-11 resulted in the creation of the Department of Homeland Security.

Giuliani, Bush and 911 Firefighter

Three days after the attacks, Bush visited Ground Zero and met with Mayor Rudy Giuliani, firefighters, police officers, and volunteers. Bush addressed the gathering via a megaphone while standing on rubble: "I can hear you. The rest of the world hears you. And the people who knocked these buildings down will hear all of us soon."

After September 11, Bush announced a global war on terror. The Afghan Taliban regime was not forthcoming with Osama bin Laden, so Bush ordered the invasion of Afghanistan to overthrow the Taliban regime. In his January 29, 2002, State of the Union Address, he asserted that an "axis of evil" consisting of North Korea, Iran, and Iraq was "arming to threaten the peace of the world" and "pose a grave and growing danger." The Bush Administration asserted both a right and the intention to wage preemptive war. This became the basis for the Bush Doctrine which weakened the unprecedented levels of international and domestic support for the United States which had followed the September 11 attacks.

He signed the Patriot Act to authorize surveillance of suspected terrorists. In 2003 Bush ordered an invasion of Iraq which began the Iraq War, falsely arguing that the Saddam Hussein regime possessed weapons of mass destruction.

In his 2004 bid for re-election, Bush commanded broad support in the Republican Party, defeating Democrat John Kerry. Bush and the Republican platform emphasized a strong commitment to the wars in Iraq and Afghanistan, support for the USA Patriot Act, a renewed shift in policy for constitutional amendments banning abortion and same-sex marriage, reforming Social Security to create private investment accounts, creation of an ownership society, and opposing mandatory carbon emissions controls. Bush also called for the implementation of a guest worker program for immigrants, which was criticized by conservatives.

John Kerry

In the election, Bush carried thirty-one of fifty states, receiving 286 electoral votes. He won an absolute majority of the popular vote, 50.7 percent to his opponent's 48.3 percent.

Over an eight-year period, Bush's once-high approval ratings steadily declined, while his disapproval numbers increased significantly.

In December 2007, the United States entered the longest post–World War II recession, caused by a housing market correction, a subprime mortgage crisis, soaring oil prices, and other factors. In February 2008, sixty-three thousand jobs were lost, a five-year record, and in November, over five hundred thousand jobs were lost, which marked the largest loss of jobs in the United States in thirty-four years. The Bureau of Labor Statistics reported that in the last four months of 2008, 1.9 million jobs were lost. By the end of 2008, the US had lost 2.6 million jobs.

Many economists and world governments determined that the situation had become the worst financial crisis since the Great Depression. Additional regulation over the housing market would have been beneficial, according to former Federal Reserve chairman Alan Greenspan.

On December 14, 2008, Muntadhar al-Zaidi, an Iraqi journalist, threw both of his shoes at President Bush during a press conference. Bush was not injured, having ducked the pair of shoes. However, White House press secretary Dana Perino received a bruise on her face after being hit by a microphone boom knocked over by security. Al-Zaidi received a three-year prison sentence, which was reduced to one year. On September 15, 2009, he was released early for good behavior.

CHAPTER EIGHTEEN

Barack Hussein Obama II

B arack Hussein Obama II a Democrat, served as the forty-fourth president of the United States from 2009 to 2017.

First Lady Michelle, President Barack Obama,
Vice-President Joe Biden and Jill

Big Day for America, we elected its first Black President!

"I was personally very happy when Obama became the president and thought it would bring an end to racism."

Obama is the only president born outside the contiguous forty-eight states. Barack Hussein Obama II was born on August 4, 1961, in Honolulu. His first name in Swahili means: "one who is blessed." Obama's father, Barack Hussein Obama Sr., was from Kenya, his mother, Stanley Ann Dunham, was from Kansas; she was mostly of English descent. Obama's father had been married in Kenya and left a pregnant wife when he and Ann met in 1960 in a Russian language class at the University of Hawaii at Manoa, where his father was a foreign student on a scholarship. The couple married in Wailuku, Hawaii, on February 2, 1961, six months before Obama was born.

In late August 1961, a few weeks after he was born, Ann took Barack and moved to Seattle, where they lived for a year. During that time, Barack's father completed his undergraduate degree in economics in Hawaii. He left to attend graduate school on a scholarship at Harvard University.

Obama's parents divorced in March 1964. Obama Sr. visited his son in Hawaii only once, at Christmas 1971, before he was killed in an automobile accident in 1982, when Obama was twenty-one years old. Recalling his early childhood, Obama said, "his father looked nothing like the people around him, that he was black as pitch, and his mother was white as milk."

In 1963 Dunham met Lolo Soetoro at the University of Hawaii. He was an Indonesian East-West Center graduate student in geography. The couple married on Molokai on March 15, 1965. After one-year, Lolo returned to Indonesia in 1966. Ann and Barack followed sixteen months later in 1967. They lived in a wealthier neighborhood in Central Jakarta. In his school record at St. Francis of Assisi Catholic Elementary School, Obama was enrolled as "Barry Soetoro" and was wrongly recorded as an Indonesian citizen and a Muslim.

As a result of his four years in Jakarta, Barack was able to speak Indonesian fluently as a child. During his time in Indonesia, Obama's stepfather taught him to be resilient and gave him "a pretty hardheaded assessment of how the world works."

Barack and his mother

In 1971 Barack returned to Honolulu to live with his maternal grandparents, Madelyn and Stanley Dunham. He attended Punahou School, a private college preparatory school, with the aid of a scholarship from fifth grade until he graduated from high school in 1979. In his youth, Barack went by the nickname "Barry." Barry lived with his mother and half-sister, Maya Soetoro in Hawaii for three years from 1972 to 1975 while his mother was a graduate student in anthropology at the University of Hawaii. Barry chose to stay in Hawaii when his mother and half-sister returned to Indonesia in 1975. His mother spent the next twenty years in Indonesia. She divorced Lolo in 1980. Ann earned a PhD degree in 1992. She died in 1995 in Hawaii following unsuccessful treatment for ovarian and uterine cancer.

Barry was a member of the "choom gang," a self-named group of friends who used alcohol, cocaine, and a lot of marijuana during his teenage years. After graduating from high school in 1979, Barack moved to LA to attend Occidental College on a full scholarship.

In 1981 Barack transferred to Columbia University in New York City as a junior, where he majored in political science with a specialty in international relations and in English literature. He graduated with a BA degree in 1983. He had a 3.7 GPA at

Columbia. Obama graduated *magna cum laude* from Harvard Law in 1991.

Obama met Trinity United Church of Christ pastor **Jeremiah Wright** in October 1987 and became a member of Trinity in 1992.

Jeremiah Wright

Obama became a civil rights attorney and an academic, teaching constitutional law at the University of Chicago Law School from 1992 to 2004. Turning to elected politics, he represented the thirteenth district in the Illinois Senate from 1997 until 2004, when he ran for the US Senate. Obama received national attention in 2004 with his March Senate primary win, his well-received July Democratic National Convention keynote address, and his landslide November election to the Senate.

Michelle

In June 1989, Obama met Michelle Robinson when he was employed as a summer associate at the Chicago law firm of Sidley Austin. Robinson was assigned for three months as Obama's adviser at the firm, and she joined him at several group social functions but declined his initial requests to date. They began dating late that summer, became engaged in 1991, and were married on October 3, 1992. Pastor Wright officiated at the wedding ceremony of Barack and Michelle Obama. After suffering a miscarriage, Michelle underwent in vitro fertilization to conceive their children. The couple's first daughter, Malia Ann, was born in 1998, followed by a second daughter, Natasha, "Sasha," in 2001. Pastor Wright baptized their children. Oprah Winfrey was also a member of Wrights congregation. Wright, on TV, made the outrageous statement, "It's not, God bless America, it's, God Damn America!" During Obama's first presidential campaign in May 2008, he resigned from Trinity after some of Wright's statements were criticized. Oprah also stopped attending Wright's church. Wright complained that Obama "threw me under the bus!" Michelle who has been mostly positive and well-liked made a statement or two she probably would like to take back. Soon after Barack became president, she said, "For the first time in my adult lifetime, I'm really proud of my country." Wright called Barack a,

"Halfrican-American president."

In 2005 the Obama family applied the proceeds of a book deal and moved from a Hyde Park, Chicago condominium to a $1.6 million house in neighboring Kenwood, Chicago. The purchase of an adjacent lot and sale of part of it to Obama by the wife of developer, campaign donor, and friend Tony Rezko, attracted media attention because of Rezko's subsequent indictment and conviction on political corruption charges that were unrelated to Obama.

In a 2006 interview, Obama highlighted the diversity of his extended family: "It's like a little mini-United Nations," he said. "I've got relatives who look like Bernie Mac, and I've got relatives who look like Margaret Thatcher." Obama has a half-sister with whom he was raised (Maya Soetoro-Ng) and seven other half-siblings from his Kenyan father's family, six of them living. Obama's mother was survived by her mother, Madelyn Dunham, until her death.

In December 2007, *Money Magazine* estimated Obama's net worth at $1.3 million. Their 2009 tax return showed a household income of $5.5 million, up from about $4.2 million in 2007 and $1.6 million in 2005, mostly from sales of his books. Per his 2012 financial disclosure, Obama may be worth as much as ten million.

In 2007 Benazir Bhutto became the first woman leader of a Muslim nation in modern history. She served two terms as prime minister of Pakistan, in 1988–90 and 1993–96. Nevertheless, in October 2007 Bhutto returned to Karachi from Dubai after eight years of self-imposed exile. Celebrations marking her return were marred by a suicide attack on her motorcade, in which numerous supporters were killed. Bhutto was assassinated in December in a similar attack while campaigning for upcoming parliamentary elections. Following her death, party leadership fell to her husband, Asif Ali Zardari, and later to their son, Bilawal Bhutto Zardari.

Benazir Bhutto

Roy and Benazir in 2007

Obama is a Protestant Christian whose religious views developed in his adult life. He wrote in *The Audacity of Hope* that he was not raised in a religious household. He described his mother, who was raised by non-religious parents, as the most spiritually awakened person he had ever known. He described his father as a "confirmed atheist" by the time his parents met, and his stepfather as "a man who saw religion as not particularly useful." Obama explained how, through working with black churches as a community organizer while in his twenties, he came to understand "the power of the African-American religious tradition to spur social change."

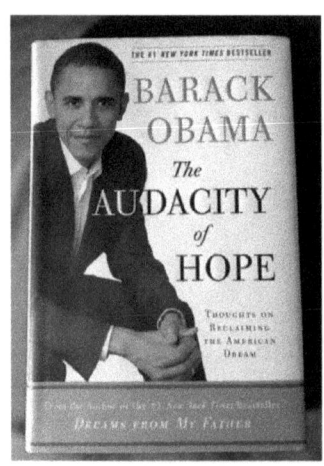

In 2008, a year after beginning his campaign, and after a close primary campaign against Hillary Clinton, he was nominated by the Democratic Party for president. Obama was elected over John McCain in the general election and was inaugurated alongside his running mate Joe Biden on January 20, 2009.

John McCain

When Obama took office he inherited a global recession, two ongoing wars and the lowest international favorability rating for the United States. President Barack Obama signed the American Recovery and Reinvestment Act (ARRA) on February 17, 2009. The Congressional Budget Office estimated it would add $787 billion in budget deficits by 2019.

The economic stimulus package helped end the Great Recession by spurring consumer spending. Most importantly, it instilled the confidence needed to boost economic growth. It also aimed to restore trust in the financial services industry. It limited bonuses for senior executives in companies that received the Troubled Asset Relief Program (TARP) funds.

Nine months later, he was named the 2009 Nobel Peace Prize laureate, a decision that drew a mixture of praise and criticism.

In 2008 and again in 2012, he was named *Time Magazine's* "Person of the Year."

Obama intervened in the troubled automotive industry in March 2009, renewing loans for General Motors (GM) and Chrysler to continue operations while reorganizing. Over the following months the White House set terms for both firms' bankruptcies, including the sale of Chrysler to Italian automaker Fiat and a reorganization of GM giving the US government a temporary 60 percent equity stake in the company.

April 2009: A plot to assassinate Obama at the Alliance of Civilizations summit in Istanbul, Turkey, was discovered after a man of Syrian origins carrying forged Al-Jazeera TV press credentials was found. The man confessed to the Turkish security services details of his plan to kill Obama with a knife. He alleged that he had three accomplices.

In June 2009, dissatisfied with the pace of economic stimulus, Obama called on his cabinet to accelerate the investment. He signed into law the Car Allowance Rebate

System, known colloquially as *Cash for Clunkers*, which temporarily boosted the economy.

On July 14, 2009, House Democratic leaders introduced a 1,017-page plan for overhauling the US health care system, which Obama wanted Congress to approve by the end of 2009. The unemployment rate rose in 2009, reaching a peak in October at 10 percent and averaging 10 percent in the fourth quarter.

On March 21, 2010, the Patient Protection and Affordable Care Act (ACA) passed by the Senate in December was passed in the House by a vote of 219 to 212. Obama signed the bill into law on March 23, 2010.

On September 27, 2010, Obama released a statement commenting on his religious views, saying,

> *"I'm a Christian by choice. My family weren't folks who went to church every week.*

On December 22, 2010, Obama signed the Don't Ask, Don't Tell Repeal Act of 2010, which fulfilled a promise made in the 2008 presidential campaign to end the Don't Ask, Don't Tell policy of 1993 that had prevented gay and lesbian people from serving openly in the United States Armed Forces.

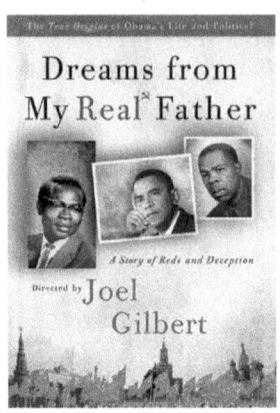

May 2011: In *Dreams from My Father,* Obama ties his mother's family history to Native American ancestors and distant relatives of slaveholder Jefferson Davis, President of the Confederate States of America during the American Civil War.

In 2011 Obama ordered the drone-strike killing of Anwar al-Awlaki, a US citizen and suspected al-Qaeda operative, leading to controversy.

Anwar al-Awlaki

In February 2011, protests in Libya began against long-time dictator Muammar Gaddafi as part of the Arab Spring. They soon turned violent. In March, as forces loyal to Gaddafi advanced on rebels across Libya, calls for a no-fly zone came from around the world, including Europe, the Arab League, and a resolution passed unanimously by the US Senate. In response to the unanimous passage of United Nations Security Council Resolution 1973 on March 17, Gaddafi—who had previously vowed to "show no mercy" to the rebels of Benghazi—announced an immediate cessation of military activities.

Muammar Gaddafi

The next day, on Obama's orders, the US military took part in air strikes to destroy the Libyan government's air defense capabilities to protect civilians and enforce a no-fly-zone, including the use of Tomahawk missiles, B-2 Spirits, and fighter jets. Six days later, on March 25, by unanimous vote of all its twenty-eight members, NATO took over leadership of the effort, dubbed Operation Unified Protector. Some Representatives questioned whether Obama had the constitutional authority to order military action in addition to questioning its cost, structure, and aftermath. Obama later expressed regret for playing a leading role in the destabilization of Libya, calling the situation there "a mess." He has stated that the lack of preparation surrounding the days following the government's overthrow was the "worst mistake" of his presidency.

On August 18, 2011, several months after the start of the Syrian Civil War, Obama issued a written statement that said: "The time has come for President Assad to step aside." This stance was reaffirmed in November 2015. In 2012 Obama authorized multiple programs run by the CIA and the Pentagon to train anti-Assad rebels. The Pentagon-run program was later found to have failed and was formally abandoned in October 2015.

In November 2011, twenty-one-year-old Oscar Ramiro Ortega-Hernandez was influenced by conspiracy theories and fringe religious viewpoints to attempt to murder Obama. Having traveled from his native Idaho, he hit the White House with several rounds fired from a semi-automatic rifle. No one was injured, but a window was broken. He was sentenced to twenty-five years in prison.

During 2011 – 2012, the far-right terrorist group FEAR plotted to carry out a series of terror attacks which included assassinating Obama. The plot was foiled when four members of the group were arrested on murder charges and one, Michael Burnett, agreed to co-operate with authorities in return for a lighter sentence.

On May 9, 2012, shortly after the official launch of his campaign for re-election as president, Obama said his views had evolved, and he publicly affirmed his personal support for the legalization of same-sex marriage, becoming the first sitting US president to do so.

In October 2012 a mentally ill man named Mitchell Kusick was arrested after confessing to his therapist that he intended to kill Obama with a shotgun at a campaign stop in Boulder, Colorado.

In April 2013, another attempt was made when a letter laced with ricin, a toxin, was sent to Obama.

After winning re-election by defeating Republican opponent Mitt Romney, Obama was sworn in for a second term on January 20, 2013.

In the wake of a chemical weapons attack in Syria, formally blamed by the Obama administration on the Assad government, Obama chose not to enforce the "red line" he had pledged and, rather than authorize the promised military action against Assad, went along with the Russia-brokered deal that led to Assad giving up chemical weapons; however attacks with chlorine gas continued.

Starting with information received from Central Intelligence Agency operatives in July 2010, the CIA developed intelligence over the next several months that determined what they believed to be the hideout of Osama bin Laden. He was living in seclusion in a large compound in Abbottabad, Pakistan, a suburban area thirty-five miles from Islamabad.

Osama bin Laden

CIA head Leon Panetta reported this intelligence to President Obama in March 2011. Meeting with his national security advisers over the course of the next six weeks, Obama rejected a plan to bomb the compound and authorized a "Surgical raid" to be conducted by United States Navy SEALs. The operation took place on May 1, 2011. Joe Biden opposed the raid. The raid resulted in the shooting death of bin Laden and the seizure of papers, computer drives and disks from the compound. DNA testing was one of five methods used to positively identify bin Laden's corpse, which was buried at sea several hours later. Within minutes of the president's announcement from Washington, DC, late in the evening on May 1, there were spontaneous celebrations around the country as crowds gathered outside the White House, and at New York City's Ground Zero and Times Square. Reaction to the announcement was positive across party lines, including from former presidents Bill Clinton and George W. Bush.

At around 4:00 a.m. on September 12, a group launched a mortar attack against a CIA annex at Benghazi, Libya, killing two CIA contractors Tyrone Woods and Glen Doherty and wounding ten others. Initial analysis by the CIA, repeated by top government officials, indicated that the attack spontaneously arose from a protest. Subsequent investigations showed that the attack was premeditated, although rioters and looters not originally part of the group may have joined in after the attacks began.

Four career State Department officials were criticized for denying requests for additional security at the facility prior to the attack. Eric J. Boswell, the Assistant Secretary of State for Diplomatic Security, resigned under pressure, while three others were suspended. In her role as Secretary of State, Hillary Clinton subsequently took responsibility for the security lapses.

January 21, 2013, Obama became the first US president in office to call for full equality for gay Americans, and the first time that a president mentioned gay rights or the word "gay" in an inaugural address.

In November 2013, the Obama administration opened negotiations with Iran to prevent it from acquiring nuclear weapons, which included an interim agreement. Negotiations took two years with numerous delays, with a deal being announced on July 14, 2015. The deal titled the "Joint Comprehensive Plan of Action" saw sanctions removed in exchange for measures that would prevent Iran from producing nuclear weapons. While Obama hailed the agreement as being a step towards a more hopeful world, the deal drew strong criticism from Republican and conservative quarters, and from Israeli Prime Minister Benjamin Netanyahu.

In addition, the transfer of $1.7 billion in cash to Iran shortly after the deal was announced was criticized by the republican party. The Obama administration said that the payment in cash was because of the "effectiveness of US and international sanctions." In order to advance the deal, the Obama administration shielded Hezbollah from the Drug

Enforcement's Project Cassandra regarding drug smuggling and from the CIA.

In 2013 the United States Internal Revenue Service (IRS) revealed that it had selected political groups applying for tax-exempt status for intensive scrutiny based on their names or political themes. Lois Lerner, who heads the IRS division that had conducted these illegal activities, that no high-level officials knew about it. The NPR Inspector General reported that Lerner had been lying. Afterward she invoked her Fifth Amendment right to remain silent. After being paid on leave for four months, Lerner retired with full pension.

After Russia's invasion of Crimea in 2014, military intervention in Syria in 2015, and the interference in the 2016 US presidential election, Obama's Russia policy was widely seen as a failure. George Robertson, a former UK defense secretary and NATO secretary-general, said Obama had "allowed Putin to jump back on the world stage and test the resolve of the West," adding that the legacy of this disaster would last.

In December 2014, after the secret meetings, it was announced that Obama, with Pope Francis as an intermediary, had negotiated a restoration of relations with Cuba, after nearly sixty years of détente. Popularly dubbed the Cuban Thaw, *The New Republic* deemed the Cuban Thaw to be "Obama's finest foreign policy achievement."

During his second inaugural address on

July 1, 2015, President Obama announced that formal diplomatic relations between Cuba and the United States would resume, and embassies would be opened in Washington and Havana. The countries' respective "interests' sections" in one another's capitals were upgraded to embassies on July 20 and August 13, 2015, respectively. Obama visited Havana, Cuba for two days in March 2016, becoming the first sitting US president to arrive since Calvin Coolidge in 1928.

In 2016, the Pentagon ended the policy that barred transgender people from serving openly in the military. The Obama administration issued a directive requiring public schools to permit transgender students to use bathrooms and locker rooms consistent with their chosen gender identity.

In December 2016, Obama permanently banned new offshore oil and gas drilling in most United States-owned waters in the Atlantic and Arctic Oceans using the 1953 Outer Continental Shelf Act.

Obama nominated three justices to the Supreme Court: Sonia Sotomayor and Elena Kagan were confirmed as justices, while Merrick Garland was denied hearings or a vote from the Republican-majority Senate.

Barack and Michelle Obama bought a home on Martha's Vineyard on October 29, 2019.

Obama's most significant legacy is generally considered to be the Affordable Care Act (ACA), provisions of which went into effect from 2010 to 2020. Many attempts by Senate Republicans to repeal the ACA, including a "skinny repeal," have thus far failed; however, in 2017 the penalty for violating the individual mandate was repealed effective 2019. Together with the Health Care and Education Reconciliation Act amendment, it represents the US healthcare system's most significant regulatory overhaul and expansion of coverage since the passage of Medicare and Medicaid in 1965. Many Americans were very upset by statements made by Obama while gaining acceptance for ACA, commonly known as "ObamaCare." He promised, "If you like your present insurance plan you can keep it!" and "If you like your doctor, you can keep your doctor." Both statements were untrue.

During Obama's presidency, a record 3.2 million people were deported from the United States. His record deportations earned Obama the nickname "Deporter in Chief." In February 2020, Biden called the deportation of hundreds of thousands of people without criminal records under the Obama administration a "big mistake."

Obama left office in January 2017 with a 60 percent approval rating. A 2018 survey of historians by the American Political Science Association ranked Obama the eighth-greatest American president.

"Barack was a great father and a good family man. He and Michelle were very well liked when he left office."

CHAPTER NINETEEN

Donald J. Trump

Donald J. Trump becomes President of the U.S.

B orn and raised in Queens, New York City, Trump graduated from the Wharton School of the University of Pennsylvania with a bachelor's degree in 1968. He became president of his father Fred Trump's real estate business in 1971 and renamed it "The Trump Organization." **The Trump Organization** is a group of about five hundred business entities of which Donald Trump is the sole or principal owner. Around 250 of these entities use the Trump name.

Donald

Trump expanded the company's operations to building and renovating skyscrapers, hotels, casinos, and golf courses. He later started various side ventures, mostly by licensing his name. From 2004 to 2015, he co-produced and hosted the reality television series The Apprentice.

In 2005 Donald married Melania Knuass, and she gave birth to their son Barron in 2006. Later that year, Melania became an American naturalized citizen. She is an intelligent and beautiful First Lady who speaks five languages.

Melania

When Donald J. Trump came down the escalator in Trump Towers in 2016 and announced that he was going to run for the presidency, I told my sons to find where I can bet on him, "I'll wage five grand in a heartbeat." The odds against him becoming the President of the United States were two hundred to one. I was told you can't bet on the presidential race in America. I would have made a million. Knowing I am not a Republican, my son's asked me what I knew about him and why I would bet on him. Here was my answer, "You don't become a billionaire without being very smart. I've only known one billionaire in my life, and he is the hardest working person, I've ever known. He worked all the time and almost never slept, maybe four hours a night. He was full of energy."

Looking at what America needed in a leader at the time, it was my opinion we needed "Dirty Harry," and Trump was "Dirty Harry!" Being a leader is somewhat like being an officer of the law. Most of the time they can be a charming, helpful friend, but, when they face an opponent with a weapon, they must become very strong like "Dirty Harry!" I believed Trump was strong enough to deal with ISIS and other terrorists who wish to hurt us, and he is a very strong and proven successful businessman who could deal with China, Russia and Kim Jong-Un.

Since Trump is such a recent president and a candidate for president number forty-seven in 2024, I'm going to just speak to all the GOOD he did to make America great again when he was president.

Donald J. Trump was elected in a surprising upset victory over Democratic nominee Hillary Clinton while losing the popular vote, becoming the first US president with no prior military or governmental office service.

In a dictatorship when a new leader takes over, they often kill-off all their opponents. In a Democracy when a new presidency takes over their opposition goes to work opposing their every move. In America the Republicans and the Democrats have been fighting for control of the country since the Declaration of Independence was signed on July 4, 1776.

The Declaration of Independence states that Americans are endowed by their Creator with certain unalienable Rights, that among these are Life, Liberty, and the pursuit of Happiness. What it didn't state was how far the losing party in an election could go in an attempt to destroy the winner. The Democrats began its onslaught of President Trump the day he took office. Not since the sixteenth President of the United States, Abraham Lincoln, and certainly, no president in my lifetime has been the target of such an attack! And of course, it was a Democrat, John Wilkes Booth who assassinated a

Republican, Abraham Lincoln in 1865 at the Ford theater in Washington DC.

Michael Thomas Flynn is a retired, three star United States Army Lieutenant General who spent thirty-three years serving his country honorably and was the twenty-fifth US National Security Advisor for the first twenty-two days of the Trump administration. General Flynn was the first causality of the Mueller investigation.

General Flynn

Special Counsel Robert Mueller investigative team member Peter Strzok called presidential candidate Donald Trump an "idiot" and "awful" and wrote that Hillary Clinton "should win 100,000,000 to 0" in text messages to an FBI lawyer, Lisa Page, with whom he was allegedly having an affair.

Lisa Page and Peter Strzok

"Trump's not ever going to become president, right? Right?!" the lawyer, Lisa Page, wrote to Strzok, according to the *Post*. "No. No he won't. We'll stop it!", Strzok responded, the Post says the IG report reveals. The text was sent in August 2016 only a few months before the presidential election, and after the FBI had started its investigation into Trump campaign aides, according to *the Post*.

In other controversy to hit Justice, Bruce Ohr, an associate attorney general with the US Department of Justice, was demoted in December 2017 because of contacts he allegedly had with the controversial Fusion GPS firm that hired the former British spy who developed the infamous "Trump dossier" on Russia. His wife, Nellie Ohr, has now become part of the controversy. Fusion GPS, a firm of former journalists, has been embroiled in national controversy since it emerged that the opposition research company hired Christopher Steele, the former spy who produced the dossier of salacious and unverified allegations about Trump. It's now been revealed that Bruce Ohr's wife, Nellie Ohr, "worked for Fusion GPS during the 2016 election." She has written on Russian-related subjects, according to Fox. When it came to light in January 2017, just days before Donald Trump took office, the so-called

Steele dossier landed like a bombshell and sent shockwaves around the world with its salacious allegations about Trump and his supposed ties to Russia. The central allegations, that Trump conspired with the Kremlin to win the 2016 election and that Russia had compromising information on him, were given a veneer of credibility because they originated from a retired British spy, Christopher Steele, who had a solid reputation.

Bruce and Nellie Ohr

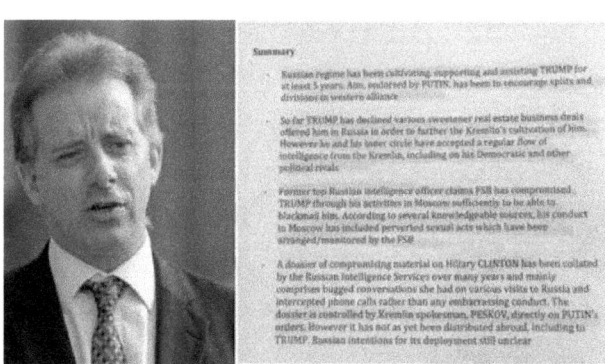

Christopher Steel and his "Trump dossier"

The dossier was part of an "opposition research project" underwritten by Democrats. Nearly a year passed before the full truth came out about the financing: The money flowed from Hillary Clinton's presidential campaign to law firm Perkins Coie, to the research company Fusion GPS, and then ultimately to Steele, who got $168,000.

Nellie Ohr worked for GPS, and her job was to gather negative information on Donald Trump from Christopher Steel. And, of course, GPS was paid for by Trumps opponent Hillary Clinton. Nellie Ohr passed information she received to her husband Bruce Ohr who was number two at the FBI. Legitimate questions are now being raised about the dossier, how it was used by Democrats as a political weapon against Trump, how it was handled by the FBI and US intelligence agencies, and how it was portrayed in the mainstream media.

An internal Justice Department review has now fully unspooled the behind-the-scenes role that some Democrats played in this saga. They paid for the research, funneled information to Steele's sources, and then urged the FBI to investigate Trump's connections to Russia. Some of the material Steele put in his memos was Russian disinformation. Steel's final and most consequential claim, that Trump's campaign worked hand-in-hand with the Kremlin, was essentially debunked by special counsel Robert Mueller's sweeping investigation.

Before the dossier, investigators already considered applying for a warrant under the Foreign Intelligence Surveillance Act, FISA, to wiretap Carter Page's communications, but they weren't sure if they could establish probable cause.

The dossier's explosive claims about Page's alleged meetings during his recent trip to Moscow "pushed it over" the line, a lawyer involved in the case told the Justice Department watchdog.

Carter Page

The FBI included snippets of Steele's reporting in the FISA application. The secretive FISA court approved the warrant in October 2016, as well as three subsequent renewal requests, meaning Page was wiretapped for about one year.

The inspector general examined the FBI's handling of the FISA applications and found that there were widespread mistakes, omissions, and errors that deeply undermined the integrity of the process. In response, the Justice Department declared that the final two FISA warrants against Page were legally invalid.

And then comes the infamous claim that Russia possessed a compromising tape of Trump with prostitutes in Moscow, which became known as the "pee tape." (Trump and Russia both denied the allegations.) According to a sub-source of the Steel dossier Igor Danchenko, he alleged he received a call from

Belarusian reporter Sergei Millian alleging a Trump/Russia conspiracy. Millian has long denied placing this call. This call was important because it was the basis, in part, of the FISA warrants against Carter Page.

US attorney John Durham's Danchenko investigation revealed Danchenko "never received such a phone call or such information" from Millian. Durham alleges that Danchenko the Steele source and the Democrat "PR Executive" (Dolan) worked together to gather intel/dirt on Trump. The Democrat PR Executive (Dolan) later admitted to the FBI he fabricated this information to Danchenko. Danchenko wasn't necessarily a source he was a go-between, providing Steele with information from the Democrat PR Executive (Dolan).

The FISA warrants were signed by FBI Director James Comey and contained information from the Steel dossier and **Comey knew the warrants were not verified.**

A FISA Warrant is a warrant to wiretap someone suspected of spying with or for a foreign government is issued by the Foreign Intelligence Surveillance Court. The court is a tribunal whose actions are carried out in secret. The tribunal has the authority to grant warrants for electronic surveillance. The court has eleven members, all federal judges. The judges serve seven-year terms. The chief justice of the US Supreme court selects the judges.

All FISA documents must be verified.

In May 2017, Deputy Attorney General Rod Rosenstein appointed Robert Mueller, a former director of the FBI, special counsel for the Department of Justice (DOJ) ordering him to "examine any links and/or coordination between the Russian government and the Trump's campaign."

Robert Mueller

Mueller established that members of the Trump campaign did not conspire or coordinated with Russian election interference activities.

When Mueller testified, everyone could see what Team Trump had seen. It wasn't pretty. And it ended Democratic hopes of turning the Russia probe into a glorious victory.

After he pressured Ukraine to investigate Hunter Biden in 2019, Congress impeached Trump for abuse of power and obstruction of Congress in December. The Senate acquitted him of both charges in February 2020.

On January 13, 2021, the Congress impeached Trump a second time, for incitement of insurrection. The Senate acquitted him on February 13, after he had already left office.

Trump was acquitted of both charges by the Republican Senate majority, 52-48 on abuse of power and 53-47 on obstruction of Congress.

Trump is the only federal officeholder in American history to have been impeached twice.

And then the **January 6 Committee,** which in my opinion was the third impeachment try by the Democrats.

Oh, by the way, if your math was correct, the answer to the earlier question on page 82 was,

A grey elephant from Georgia.

How did I know that you ask? Let's try it again! Pick a number between one and ten. Now double your number. Now add six. Now divide by two. Now subtract your original number and your answer is three!

So, what is my point?

If you have control of the input information you can to a great degree control the outcome.

So, be careful when you choose your source of information. If you believe that the news media, television, newspapers, radio, the internet are neutral platforms, you may have your head in the sand. What we get from our so-called news souses are "Opinions with a Purpose", their purpose, not ours. We all want a level playing field, not the allusion of fairness. We must always ask, "Is the jury fair or is it one-sided?" I will give you a few cases where I believe the jury was one-sided.

Gil Garcetti

The criminal trial of former college and NFL football star O.J. Simpson, who was acquitted in 1995 of the murder of his ex-wife Nicole Brown Simpson and her friend Ronald Goldman. It was one of the most notorious criminal trials in American history. I watched every minute of the OJ trial and said, "When LA District Attorney Gil Garcetti charged Simpson in downtown Los Angeles, as opposed to Brentwood, in which jurisdiction the crimes took place, the outcome changed." In Brentwood, the jury would have been mostly white. In downtown LA it resulted in a jury pool that was less educated, had lower incomes, and contained more Black Americans.

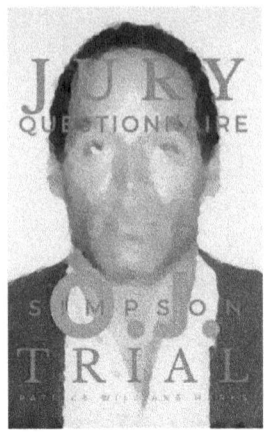

The jury was made up of four males and eight females. Eight of the jurors were Black, one Hispanic, only one white person and two mixed races. Robert Shapiro was Simpson's lead attorney. Belief in Simpson's innocence or guilt was divided largely along racial lines, with a majority of African Americans in support of Simpson and most white Americans believing in his guilt.

Roy with Robert Shapiro

In another more recent case, Former Hillary Clinton's campaign lawyer Michael Sussmann was acquitted for lying to the FBI when he handed over since-debunked computer data that purportedly tied Donald Trump to Russia, with jurors drawn from a largely Democrat-leaning pool saying special counsel John Durham didn't prove the case beyond a reasonable doubt even though Sussmann admitted he lied.

John Durham   Michael Sussmann

In a town where over 92 percent of voters cast their ballot for Clinton, it's difficult to find potential jurors who didn't support her. (According to data from Politico, Clinton received 92.8 percent of the 2016 vote in the District of Columbia vs. 4.1 percent for Republican Donald Trump.)

Sussmann's trial was overseen by federal Judge Christopher Cooper, who was nominated by former President Barack Obama. Cooper's wife represented former FBI lawyer Lisa Page, the anti-Trump alleged lover of former FBI agent Peter Strzok. And Cooper himself described Sussmann as a "professional acquaintance" with whom he had worked at the Department of Justice during the 1990s.

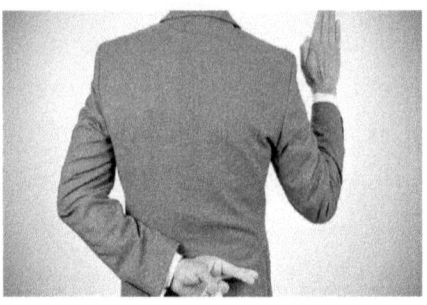

I swear to be truthful!

Attorney General Merrick Garland officiated at Cooper's May 1999 wedding.

In one instance during jury selection, Cooper overruled prosecutors' objections to seating a man who had donated to Clinton's 2016 presidential campaign, noting the prospective juror had "expressed a high degree of confidence" that he could be impartial. Three jurors were Clinton donors, and a fourth was a donor to Democratic Rep. Alexandria Ocasio-Cortez of New York. A fifth juror revealed that her daughter and Sussmann's daughter were on the same sports team. The Durham team objected to this juror, but the presiding judge, Cooper, overruled it.

What do you think? Was that a fair, impartial jury?

One of the more stunning revelations from the trial came courtesy of Clinton's own campaign manager, Robby Mook. His testimony proved the truth of Durham's overall case – that Hillary personally approved the plot to leak key parts of the collusion story to the press. "Plausible Deniability" is no longer a defense for Hillary Clinton.

And how do feel about the January 6th committee? As president, Trump authorized twenty thousand National Guardsmen to protect the Capitol on January 4th. Speaker Nancy Pelosi who is responsible for the protection of the Capitol turned down Trumps offer. All members of the January 6th committee were selected by democrat Nancy Pelosi. The committee is made up of seven Democrats and two Republicans. All members, including the two Republicans, voted to impeach President Trump. The committee had **no defensive** side. During the trial, "hearsay testimony" was accepted as forensic evidence. In politics, there is no such thing as a fair fight. One-sided justice is never fair.

Insurrection?

Why did the Democrats label the January 6 riot an insurrection? What does the word mean and what was their plan?

Ever since a mob stormed the U.S. Capitol after attending a Trump-headlined "Stop the Steal" rally on Jan. 6, 2021, there has been a debate over whether to call the event an "insurrection." On January 6th hundreds of rally attendees, a few armed with metal flagpoles and baseball bats, smashed their way into the Capitol building and loitered in the halls. An "insurrection," by definition, is a "violent uprising against an authority or government." Was the crowd truly violent? This distinction determines whether those who breached the Capitol are to be accurately described as "rally goers" or "rioters," "patriots" or "terrorists," "peaceful protestors" or "insurrectionists." An Insurrection is an organized attempt by a group of people to take over their government and take control of their country by violence.

To start with on January 4th President Trump offered 20,000 National Guardsmen to protect the capitol from harm. Both Nancy Pelosi who was in charge of the capitol police and Muriel Bowser who was in charge of the Washington DC police turned him down.

Trumps "Stop the Steal" speech was protected by our first amendment.

It is my belief that the January 6th (so called) insurrection was planned and directed by the Democrat Party

They can't say Donald Trump was trying to take over the country that, as the President he was already in control of.

What did Trump do that was GOOD for America?

Trump says he has never drunk alcohol, smoked cigarettes, or used drugs and that he sleeps about four or five hours a night. Nice to know the president is sober when he makes important decisions that may cost lives.

President Trump receives non-stop criticism in the press. I agree that criticism is necessary when a president makes mistakes, but it's unfair to always criticize and never recognize any of the good things a president has done. It might be a refreshing change to recall some of the remarkable, nation-changing good things that Trump accomplished for America in his effort to "MAKE AMERICA GREAT AGAIN." Here is my personal list. When Trump became president, one of our greatest fears was ISIS. ISIS was founded by Abu Bakr al-Baghdadi, an Iraqi. ISIL (Islamic State of Iraq and the Levant) is a Sunni jihadist group with a particularly violent ideology that calls itself a caliphate and claims religious authority over all Muslims. President Trump gave our military forces the freedom to defeat ISIS and drive them out of large sections of Iraq and Syria, which they did. Under President Trump's leadership, US military forces located and killed ISIS founder and terrorist leader Abu Bakr al-Baghdadi on Oct. 27, 2019. President Trump also directed the killing of Iranian terrorist mastermind Qassem Soleimani on Jan. 2, 2020.

Abu Bakr al-Baghdadi   Oassem Soleimani

President Trump has increased **military spending** by nearly $150 billion per year from $605 billion in 2016 to $750 billion, steadily rebuilding US military readiness.

Reversing President Obama's repeated marginalization and shunning of Israel, President Trump has reaffirmed our commitment to support and defend Israel. He decisively moved the United States Embassy from Tel Aviv to Jerusalem. He recognized the Golan Heights as part of Israel. He welcomed Prime Minister Benjamin Netanyahu to the White House several times and repeatedly reaffirmed our support for Israel. Recently, there was an article in the *Jerusalem Post* stating that Israel has never had a better friend in the White House than Donald Trump.

Netanyahu

On August 13, 2020, President Trump announced that **Israel and the United Arab Emirates** (UAE) had come to a historic agreement to establish full diplomatic relations between the two countries, including the establishment of permanent embassies and the beginning of direct airline flights between the two countries. This was a monumental change in the Middle East.

President Trump has insisted that NATO countries start to **pay their fair share** of defense costs, and some NATO countries have responded by increasing their defense budgets. NATO was designed to protect European countries from Russia and those countries not only were not paying their agreed amount, but they were also buying their oil from Russia, making Russia stronger.

President Trump has negotiated **new trade agreements** with Mexico, Canada, and China, and all of them give more favorable treatment to the United States than the previous treaties did. The United States-Mexico-Canada Agreement (USMCA) became effective in July 2020 as the successor to NAFTA.

Whereas President Obama sent only humanitarian aid, President Trump authorized the selling of actual **military equipment to Ukraine**, including Javelin missiles that were necessary to defend against Russian aggression.

Trump has been the first president to decisively denounce China's blatant practice of **industrial espionage and bullying, stealing of intellectual property**, and violating international copyright protections. He has followed up with strong trade sanctions against China, an increased US naval presence in the South China Sea, and the closing of the Chinese consulate in Houston, which was a center of Chinese espionage.

President Trump has relentlessly battled against Democratic stonewalling and liberal federal judges to build an effective,

secure border wall along more than two hundred miles of our southern border, and it could have reached as much as 450 miles by the end of 2020, had he stayed in office.

Trump signed the **Tax Cuts and Jobs Act of 2017**, which cut taxes for individuals and businesses and rescinded the individual health insurance mandate penalty of the Affordable Care Act. Trump's extensive canceling of excessive government regulations on businesses have given a tremendous boost to the American economy. On January 30, 2017, Trump signed Executive Order 13771, which directed that for every new regulation administrative agencies issue **at least two prior regulations be identified for elimination.**

An estimated twenty-five thousand pages of regulations have been canceled, resulting in a savings of $3,100 per household per year. Another result of tax cuts combined with deregulation has been the addition of thousands of new jobs, so that unemployment (before the coronavirus crisis) fell to the lowest point in fifty years, and unemployment among African-American and Hispanic workers was the lowest it has ever been in history.

ENERGY INDEPENDENCE: President Trump gave approval to the Keystone pipeline, the Dakota access pipeline, and oil production from the Alaska National Wildlife Refuge, a vast uninhabited region that could produce up to 20 percent of our petroleum needs. His administration has also granted more permits for mining of oil, gas, and coal from federal lands. The result has been lower energy prices (which benefits everyone) and also US energy independence so that we were now becoming the leading exporter rather than a net importer of energy.

Reforming the Department of Veterans Affairs: On June 23, 2017, President Trump signed the Veterans Accountability and Whistleblower Protection Act, which gave the Secretary of Veterans Affairs streamlined authority to fire unproductive employees and to appoint new medical directors at VA hospitals. But even before that law, the Trump administration had begun to clean house, and over five hundred employees were fired from the Veterans Administration in the first six months of Trump's presidency.

Criminal justice reform: President Trump signed the First Step Act on December 21, 2018. This law gives judges more flexibility in reducing mandatory sentencing guidelines in individual cases, eliminates the "three strikes" requirement of life imprisonment for some offenses, improves opportunities for academic and vocational education within prisons, provides more support for the successful reentry of released prisoners into society, and requires prisoners to be placed in prisons near their place of primary residence where possible.

Reducing prescription drug prices: On July 24, 2020, President Trump signed four executive orders aimed at reducing prescription drug prices. Trump was working to stop pharmaceutical companies from selling their drugs to Americans at higher prices. He believed Americans should not be subsidizing the costs of drugs for foreign countries.

In 2017, when **North Korea's** nuclear weapons were increasingly seen as a serious threat, Trump escalated his rhetoric, warning that North Korean aggression would be met with "fire and fury like the world has never seen." In 2017 Trump declared that he wanted North Korea's "complete denuclearization," and engaged in name-calling with leader Kim Jong-un. After this period of tension, Trump and Kim exchanged at least twenty-seven letters in which the two men described a warm personal friendship.

Trump appointed three Supreme Court justices to

Neil Gorsuch　　Brett Kavanaugh　　Amy Coney Barrett

The Supreme Court. All are committed to interpreting the Constitution and laws according to the original meaning of the words, rather than according to what a modern liberal judge thinks the law should have said.

Trump appointed 226 Article III federal judges, including fifty-four federal appellate judges. Senate Republicans, led by Senate Majority Leader Mitch McConnell, rapidly confirmed Trump's judicial appointees, shifting the federal judicial to the right.

Over a million Americans died from the C-19 virus sent to us from China, and they have not been held accountable.

Trump created his **Warp Speed** system to produce two vaccines in less than a year that would normally take six to ten years. In the first ten months it resulted in saving an estimated **1.1 million American lives nationally,** including twenty thousand in California according to researchers from UC San Francisco in collaboration with the California Department of Public Health published in the journal JAMA Network Open in April 2022.

Inflation was 1.6 percent when Trump left office in January 2020. The cost of gas across the nation averaged $2.40 per gallon.

Remember: For all his sympathetic words to Jews and blacks, Roosevelt failed to deliver. For all his hostile words, Truman delivered. *Actions do speak louder than words.*

Actions prove who someone is,
words just prove who they pretend to be.

"If you judge Trump by what he said, you will probably dislike him. If, on the other hand, you judge him by what he did, you will vote for him again."

CHAPTER TWENTY

Joseph Robinette Biden Jr.

J oseph Robinette Biden Jr. is the forty-sixth and current president of the United States.

A member of the Democratic Party, he served as the forty-seventh vice president from 2009 to 2017 under President Barack Obama and was in the United States Senate from 1973 to 2009 (thirty-six years).

Biden was born in Scranton, Pennsylvania, moving with his family to New Castle County, Delaware, in 1953 when he was ten. His father, Joseph Biden Sr., worked cleaning furnaces and as a used car salesman. His mother was Catherine Eugenia "Jean" Finnegan. Joe credits his parents with instilling in him toughness, hard work, and perseverance. He has recalled his father frequently saying, "Champ, the measure of a man is not how often he is knocked down, but how quickly he gets up." When he had been bullied by one of the bigger kids in the neighborhood, his mother told him, "Bloody their nose so you can walk down the street the next day!" As a child, Joe struggled with a stutter, and kids called him "Dash" to mock him. He eventually overcame his speech impediment by memorizing long passages of poetry and reciting them aloud in front of the mirror.

Joe

Joe attended the St. Helena School until he gained acceptance into the prestigious Archmere Academy. Although he had to work by washing the school windows and weeding the gardens to help his family afford tuition, Biden had long dreamed of attending the school, which he called "the object of my deepest desire, my Oz." At Archmere, Joe was a solid student and, despite his small size, a standout receiver on the football team. Joe graduated from Archmere in 1961.

On August 27, 1966, Joe married Neilia Hunter, after overcoming her parents' reluctance for her to wed a Roman Catholic. They had three children: Joseph R. "Beau" Biden III, Robert Hunter Biden, and Naomi Christina "Amy" Biden.

Neilia

In 1968 Joe earned a Juris from Syracuse University College of Law, ranked seventy-sixth in his class of eighty-five. He acknowledged he plagiarized a law review article for a paper he wrote in his first year at law school. He was admitted to the Delaware bar in 1969.

While studying at the University of Delaware and Syracuse University, Joe obtained five student draft deferments, at a time when most draftees were sent to the Vietnam War. In 1968, based on a physical examination, he was given a conditional medical deferment; in 2008 a spokesperson for Biden said his having had "asthma as a teenager" was the reason for the deferment.

In 1972, Biden defeated Republican incumbent J. Caleb Boggs to become the junior US senator from Delaware.

On December 18, 1972, a few weeks after the election, Biden's wife Neilia and one-year-old daughter Naomi were killed in an automobile accident while Christmas shopping in Hockessin, Delaware. Neilia's station wagon was hit by a semitrailer truck as she pulled out from an intersection. Their sons Beau (aged three) and Hunter (aged two) survived the accident and were taken to the hospital in fair condition, Beau with a broken leg and other wounds and Hunter with a minor skull fracture and other head injuries.

Jill

Biden and his second wife, Jill, met in 1975 on a blind date and married in 1977. Their daughter Ashley is a social worker. She is married to physician Howard Krein. Beau Biden became an Army Judge Advocate in Iraq and later Delaware Attorney

General; he died of brain cancer in 2015. Hunter Biden is a Washington lobbyist and investment adviser.

Elected to the Senate in 1972, Biden was re-elected in 1978, 1984, 1990, 1996, 2002, and 2008, regularly receiving about 60 percent of the vote.

In February 1988, after several episodes of increasingly severe neck pain, Biden was taken by ambulance to Walter Reed Army Medical Center for surgery to correct a leaking intracranial berry aneurysm. While recuperating, he suffered a pulmonary embolism, a serious complication. After a second aneurysm was surgically repaired in May, Biden's recuperation kept him away from the Senate for seven months.

Biden formally declared his candidacy for the 1988 Democratic presidential nomination on June 9, 1987.

By August his campaign's messaging had become confused and in September, he plagiarized a speech by British Laboure Party leader Neil Kinnock.

Biden has made several false or exaggerated claims about his early life: **he lied and said that he had earned three degrees in college, that he attended law school on a full scholarship, that he had graduated in the top half of his class, and that he had marched in the civil rights movement.** Biden withdrew his candidacy, saying it had been overrun by "the exaggerated shadow" of his past mistakes. **Biden had a pattern of being a liar.** After exploring the possibility of a run in several previous cycles, in January 2007, Biden declared his candidacy in the 2008 elections. During his campaign, Biden focused on the Iraqi War, his record as chairman of major Senate committees, and his foreign-policy experience. In mid-2007, Biden stressed his foreign policy expertise compared to Obama's.

In the first contest on January 3, 2008, Biden placed fifth in the Iowa caucuses, garnering slightly less than one percent of the state delegates. He withdrew from the race that evening.

On August 22, 2008, Obama announced that Biden would be his running mate. Privately, Biden's remarks frustrated Obama. *"How many times is Biden gonna say something stupid?"* In October 2010, Biden said Obama had asked him to remain as his running mate for the 2012 presidential election.

In 2019 Biden ran in the Democratic Primary against seventeen other Democrats and won and then ran against President Donald J. Trump.

On August 11, he announced U.S. Senator Kamala Harris of California as his running mate, making her the first (half) African-American and (half) South Asian American vice-presidential nominee on a major-party ticket. Biden received seventy-nine million votes, giving him the most votes of any presidential candidate in history.

Kamala

Trump's greatest asset was the good economy and then along came the coronavirus that destroyed the American economy. Was COVID-19 an accident or on purpose? While Trump campaigned across America, Biden stayed in his basement and made very few appearances. Trump received 73.6 million votes, more than any sitting president in history, and yet he lost.

During his 2020 campaign, Biden vowed to nominate the first Black woman to the Supreme Court if a vacancy occurred, a promise he reiterated after the announcement of Breyer's retirement. In February, Biden nominated federal judge Katanji Brown Jackson to the Supreme Court. She was confirmed! When she was asked to describe what a woman was, she said, "I cannot!" Interesting! It's genetic, just look in their jeans!

On June 24, 2022, the United States Supreme Court overturned *Roe v. Wade*. This removes the 1973 landmark 5-4 decision that took abortion away from the people and gave it to the government. This June 24th decision gives it back to the people. This decision will make no difference in states, California, and New York for example, where the people want to continue without change. The people in other states may restrict or outlaw this procedure. This decision is praised by most conservatives and angered most liberals.

Zawahiri and bin Laden

Ayman Mohammed Rabie al-Zawahiri was an Egyptian-born Islamic jihadist and terrorist. Ayman al-Zawahiri worked as a surgeon. In 1985 al-Zawahiri went to Saudi Arabia on Hajj and stayed to practice medicine in Jeddah for a year. As a reportedly qualified surgeon, when his organization merged with bin Laden's al-Qaeda, he became bin Laden's personal advisor and physician. He had first met bin Laden in Jeddah in 1986. After the September 11 attacks, the United States Department of State offered a twenty-five-million dollar reward for information or intelligence leading to al-Zawahiri's capture. He became the leader of al-Qaeda in June 2011, succeeding Osama bin Laden following his killing by U.S. forces in Pakistan. Al-Zawahiri was previously a senior member of Islamist organizations that led attacks in Asia, Africa, North America, and Europe. In 2012, al-Zawahiri called on Muslims to kidnap Westerners in Muslim countries.

Ketanji Jackson

On July 31, 2022, 21 years after 9-11, a United States drone strike killed al-Zawahiri in Kabul, Afghanistan.

We are living in the Biden/Harris era, and I am sure that you are developing opinions about your future as an American.

Most of what was said about the previous presidents has been a result of research of history. I'm writing about President Biden and Vice President Harris as it happens. These are my opinions in real time. I believe "middle America" is very wide. I am involved with people as you are every day. I believe we are more together than we are apart. Politicians describe us as being at each other's throat. It appears to me they are using the "divide and conquer" approach to gaining power.

Listening to a politician make you promises is like being a bartender and listening to your patrons. It's very hard to tell who's drunk and who's stupid. And which ones are both!

A few things for you to consider. Do you agree with how each is being handled? Are the decisions smart or are they stupid? Are there decisions in the favor of the American people? Use your common sense as you analyze what is happening and not from which political party the decisions are coming.

I will tell you exactly what I think about what is going on. Once again, I am not telling you what to think about the facts, which is up to you. However, "the facts are the facts!"

Or are they? Facts do not lie, but liars lie about facts! So please, do not accept all I say. Select your best search system and find out for yourself what you believe the truth to be.

In his first action when he became president, Biden closed the Keystone pipeline, he stopped drilling for oil in ANWR, the nineteen-million-plus-acre Arctic National Wildlife Refuge in Alaska. He stopped fracking and coal production. America quickly lost its "energy independence." We now, once again, must rely on foreign countries, including China, Russia, and the Middle East for our energy. During his campaign Biden told a young lady, "Look into my eyes, I guarantee I will eliminate fossil fuel!" Do you think that was a good move on Biden's part? Do you think his actions are smart or stupid, and did they cause the rising cost of gas?

I do! If you wish to control people, "Make them poor and control their energy. You can turn their lights off!"

Are you happy with the rate of inflation effecting the cost of food, the cost of housing? We were told that taxes would not be raised on anyone earning under four hundred thousand dollars per year. Sounds good, make the rich pay more and leave the middle class and poor Americans alone. If you are still earning the same amount or 3 percent more but, the cost of everything you purchase has gone up by 10 percent, isn't the result the same as a raise in taxes? In addition to raising the price on everything the companies are reducing the size of the product they are delivering.

Biden opened the southern border to allow anyone to come into America. They are not vetted, so we don't know who they are. We don't know if they are criminals in the country from where they came. We don't know if they are bringing contagious disease. We don't know if they are drug dealers bringing fentanyl to kill our youth. Are we getting more homeless people to live on our streets in tents?

When you leave the windows open,

THE BUGS FLY IN

We must live with the problems the open borders have created which are far-reaching. Most of the illegals entering our country cannot speak our language. They have no means of support. They have no place to live. They have no medical care. Their children need education; first we must teach them English and then to read and write.

According to the FBI Terror Watchlist, there were two suspected or known terrorists caught entering the US illegally through our southern border in 2017. In 2018 it was six. In 2019 it was zero. In 2020 it was three. In 2021, after Biden took office, it jumped up to fifteen. And in the first six months of 2022, fifty suspected or known terrorists have come across our border. In the first two years of the Biden administration six times as many terrorists have crossed our border than in the last four years under Trump. The US Border Control states "that they estimate that 1,800 people come across the border every day who are not caught." You must wonder,

"When will the next '9-11' happen?"

How do you feel about how we left Afghanistan and leaving over one hundred unarmed and defenseless Americans behind?

As America left, thirteen US service members died in an attack outside of the Kabul airport. The suicide bombing also killed 170 American allied Afghans and left eighteen other US service members wounded. From the White House, Biden proclaimed, "We will not forgive. We will not forget. We will hunt you down, and make you pay!" And then an American drone strike killed innocent civilians, including children, Pentagon officials admitted. And then nothing! I guess Biden did forget.

Can you believe we left eighty-three billion dollars in military equipment for the Taliban, Al-Qaeda, and ISIS to use against us in the future? Here is a list of what we left:

- 2,000 Armored Vehicles Including Humvees and MRAPs
- 75,989 Total Vehicles: FMTV, M35, Ford Rangers, Ford F350, Ford Vans, Toyota Pickups, Armored Security Vehicles etc. 45 UH-60 Blackhawk Helicopters, 50 MD530G Scout Attack Helicopters ScanEagle Military Drone, 30 Military Version Cessnas, 4 C-130s, 29 Brazilian made A-29 Super Tucano Ground Attack

Aircraft. Heavy Equipment, Including Bull Dozers, Backhoes, Dump Trucks, Excavators.

- *=208+ Aircraft Total At* least 600,000+ Small arms M16, M249 SAWs, M24 Sniper Systems, 50 Calibers, 1,394 M203 Grenade Launchers, M134 Mini Gun, 20mm. Gatling Guns and Ammunition, 61,000 M203 Rounds, 20,040 Grenades,
- Howitzers, Mortars +1,000's of Rounds, 162,000 pieces of Encrypted Military Communications Gear,16,000+ Night Vision Goggles, Newest Technology Night Vision Scopes, Thermal Scopes and Thermal Mono Googles,
- 10,000 2.75-inch Air to Ground Rockets.
- Reconnaissance Equipment (ISR) Laser Aiming Units.
- Explosives Ordnance C-4, Semtex, Detonators, Shaped Charges, Thermite, Incendiaries, AP/API/APIT,2,520 Bombs, Administration Encrypted Cell Phones and Laptops ALL operational Pallets with Millions of Dollars in US Currency, Millions of Rounds of Ammunition including but not limited to 20,150,600 rounds of 7.62 mm. 9,000,000 rounds of 50. Caliber.
- Large Stockpile of Plate Carriers and Body Armor
- US Military HIIDE, for Handheld Interagency Identity Detection Equipment Biometrics. We could have sent all this equipment to Ukraine so they could defend themselves from the Russian invasion. Instead, we sent another hundred billion dollars to Ukraine.

Does that make sense to you?

Never in my lifetime have I seen such an embarrassing American military failure. We left Americas longest war with no plan!

Did you like how the C-19 lockdowns, that destroyed our economy, were handled?

How do you feel about the mask-uerade which at times made no sense?

Are you happy with how the crime rate is going up? We are being told to "Defund and Disarm!" Think about it. First the government wants you to get rid of the police who are there to protect us and then give up our guns so we can't protect ourselves. Does that make good sense to you?

If someone breaks into your home and you call the police it may take some time before they arrive; if you own a gun, help is just seconds away!

I believe it's better to have a gun and not need it than to need a gun and not have it!

What do you think?

Are you happy with the way our children are being schooled? Should kids in the first grade be taught about sex by someone other than their parents?

Are you happy allowing men to participate in women's sports?

The Atlanta-based agency, with a twelve- billion-dollar budget and more than eleven thousand employees, is charged with protecting Americans from disease outbreaks and other public health threats. CDC Director Dr. Rochelle Walensky admitted major COVID-19 mistakes that helped destroy the American economy. If science is to be believed, scientists cannot lie, and they did! The CDC's handling of C-19 was the biggest public failure in history. They closed the schools even though science told us our children were not at risk. The CDC cannot pay for this big failure with a simple apology.

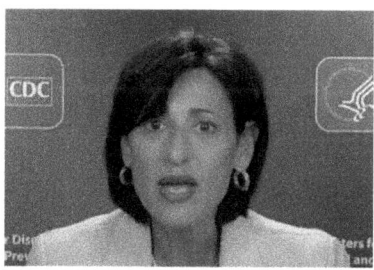

Walenski

Why were the CDC leaders not fired!

Joe and Ashley

What's your thought about **Biden's daughter's diary**? The president's daughter, Ashley moved from a half-way house where she was staying, following her arrest for drug problems, and left her diary under a mattress. And it was found by the next resident. In her diary she wrote that she thought it was inappropriate that she took showers with her father which caused her to be "sexually compulsive" for the rest of her life. She believed it caused her to be "hyper-sexualized" at a young age. These are the characteristics of a child that has been abused. Keep in mind that she was writing what she thought at the time. Any questions?

Do you think it's okay for citizens to protest outside Supreme Court Justices homes? Is it fair to give out information to the public to let protesters know where the Justices live? The **federal law**, 18 U.S. Code Section 1507, the "Picketing or Parading" law states that anyone "with the intent of interfering with, obstructing, or impeding the administration of justice, or with the intent of influencing any judge, juror, witness, or court officer in the discharge of his duty," cannot picket near a judge's residence. A conviction on this charge could come with up to a year in prison, a fine, or both. A twenty-six-year-old, Nicholas Roeske, was allegedly motivated by his anger that Kavanaugh might help overturn *Roe v. Wade*, planned to assassinate Kavanaugh and two other Supreme Court Justices.

How China is killing Americans!

The killing goes from China to Mexico to the United States.

Fentanyl is manufactured under strict control in China.

Under pressure from the U.S., Chinese suppliers have had difficulty sending the pills straight to America.

Chinese suppliers have come up with an alternative plan. These Chinese drug suppliers send the ingredients to make fentanyl to cartels in Mexico. After creating the fentanyl, either in raw powder or pill form, the cartels must get it to their customers in America.

Joe Biden does his part. Biden opens the Southern border and allows the drugs to flow into the United States.

According to US Center for Disease Control, CDC , Fentanyl was the leading cause of 107 thousand deaths due to drug overdoses for the 12-month period ending in August 2022. Presently, 300 people die from overdose every day in America. For every person who dies from overdose there are a hundred other American whose lives are ruined by these drugs.

Is President Joe Biden corrupt?

Follow the money! It is reported that the Biden Family have received **thirty-one million dollars** from China. Including the **five million dollars** that Hunter Biden received from CEFC, the Chinese oil company. Did the money influence the shutting down of the Keystone pipeline? Why did Hunter receive **$3.5 million** from the wife of the former mayor of Moscow? Why does Hunter have a stake in the Chinese private equity firm, BHR that controls **$2.1 billion** investment dollars in China? And why did Hunter get paid **eighty-three thousand dollars per month** from Burisma Energy Company in Ukraine? Why did Vice President Joe Biden demand the Ukrainian government fire the prosecutor who was investigating Burisma? Biden told the Ukrainian government if they did not fire the prosecutor, he was leaving Ukraine in six hours six hours and if the prosecutor had not been fired, they would not receive **One Billion Dollars** of foreign aid from the United States.

To quote Joe Biden, "Son of a bitch, they did it."

According to a highly creditable FBI whistleblower, document 1023 that is in FBI hands, Joe Biden, and Hunter Biden **each** received **$5 million dollars** from Burisma for forcing the Ukrainian government to fire the prosecutor who was prosecuting Burisma. Document 1023 shows that Joe got his son, Hunter the job with Burisma. Joe lied when he said, *"I have never spoken to Hunter about his business affairs!"* Doc. 1023 states that an Exec of Burisma has 17 recordings, 15 with Hunter and 2 with Joe, proving their corruption.

Has Biden set-up the Department of Justice and the FBI to go after his chief pollical rival for the 2024 presidential race?
Is that not election interference, and is America becoming a Third-World Country?

Today, oil is the lifeblood of our economy. Do you agree that we should become, once again, energy independent and not depend on countries who are often our enemies?

In the American pollical system,

"A politician is controlled by his or her supporters!"

We are being told we will be experiencing electrical blackouts this summer because there is a shortage of electricity. So, we are being told to buy electric cars and get rid of gas stoves and use electricity we don't have. Everything connected to electricity and batteries comes from China. If China wants to control Americans, they need to get control of America's energy. If American people don't do what China wants them to do, China will turn them off! Does that make sense to you?

Who came up with all these programs, seemly without a clue? Stumbling, Mumbling and Bumbling.

"It's Mr. Magoo, that's Who!"

"I believe this son of a used-car salesman is America's first Chinese President!"

On July 21,2024, Joseph R. Biden stepped down from his campaign for president in 2024.

So, now Joe is out, and Kamala is in!

It's still Communism verses FREEDOM!

The Gigglier

Same horse in the race with a different jockey. This radical jockey as the "Border Czar" has never won a race, she's on the racetrack but she's galloping in the wrong direction. She is racing against freedom! Harris selected Tim Walz as her running mate. Walz, the Governor of Minnesota, stands accused of 'stolen valor' when he claims he retired as a command sergeant major, the highest enlisted rank. He also said he carried an assault weapon at war. He was never at war.

Tim Walz

CHAPTER TWENTY-ONE

Choices, Choices, Choices

I have discovered that, in-life, our success is determined by the choices we make! If, daily, we make lousy choices, it serves to produce mediocrity or less. On the other hand, if we make good choices, they lead us to a more abundant lifestyle. Some choices are more important than others but, they all count. Every choice you make moves you closer to where you want to be or further away.

How important are your choices to you?

I don't wish to tell you how or what choices you should make. That choice is yours alone! My wish is to present to you more information on this subject so you can make better choices. Does that make sense to you?

Thus far, we have analyzed one hundred years of American presidents from 1923 to 2023. Personally, I have lived under the leadership of fifteen of those presidents, seven were Republicans and eight were Democrats, counting the president now in office. Each president of the United States was put into office by the citizens of our country. Every four years we vote for the leader of America, who is the leader of the free world. We have differing opinions of who the president should be.

"If everyone is thinking alike,

somebody isn't thinking!"

Gen. George S. Patton

Do you really love America?

The members of our military, men, and women, are willing to put their life on the line to protect the FREEDOM for all Americans. Freedom is not free, and it often comes at great cost. How about you? Would you be willing to fight to save your freedom? Are you a loyal American or an American in name only? When you vote, do you vote for the person who you believe will make decisions that are best for all Americans, or do you vote based on the groupthink of a political party with which you are affiliated? Do you make this "Very Important Choice" that will have a big effect on your future freedom and the future of your family, based on to which political party your parents belonged? No independent thought, my parents were a (Democrat or Republican) and so am I.

"You gotta listen to a lot of people, but in the end, you've gotta listen to yourself!"

Elvis Presley

When is the last time you pledged allegiance to your country? When is the last time you even thought about it? Is your loyalty to your country important? The pledge has thirty-one words which affirm the values and freedom that the American flag represents.

I pledge allegiance to the flag of the United States of America and to the Republic for which it stands, one Nation under God, indivisible, with liberty and justice for all.

Imagine you are not married, and you are in the dating process planning to choose your mate for your lifetime. A poor choice will affect your future in many negative ways.

Here are just a few attributes that I believe you would consider. Will your selected mate be a good parent for your future children? Is your selected mate charming and good looking? And is that all that matters? Remember, as people age, their charm and good looks may change. How about their "honesty and loyalty?" Would "race or color" be a deterrent? Is your selected mate "moody"? If two moody people join, it doesn't usually last. When a moody and a non-moody join, the non-moody believes they can change the moody person. They usually make it until the children grow up and then the non-moody realizes the moody will not change and they separate. I find two non-moody people are reasonable and solve problems as they come up.

Are you and your selected mate "like minded?" Is your selected mate in good health? Does he or she have a good sense of humor and a positive attitude? Is your selected mate your "best friend?" How much do they love you?

What about their "financial stability?" How about their "education and work experience?" These and many other important characteristics will influence this very important

choice. You may not find the perfect mate of your dreams, but you should get as close as you can.

Now imagine you inherited a multi-national company worth billions of dollars. You now must make another important choice. Because you may not have the skill to manage your new company, you will need to select someone to run the company for you. Would you hire a person only because they belonged to a club or group where you are a member? Would you hire a person because of their color?

Would their color be a deterrent? Would you hire a person because of their gender? Wouldn't you use an interviewing system similar to choosing your mate? A mistake will prove very costly.

With these thoughts in mind, how important is choosing the person who will become your leader, the leader of America, and the leader of the free world? What do you consider?

This is a choice you as a citizen of the United States of America, you have the privilege of making, once every four years.

The president you choose will choose the members of his or her cabinet. If you select a strong, smart leader, he or she will probably select strong, smart members of his or her cabinet.

The cabinet includes fifteen department heads as follows: Secretary of State, Secretary of Treasury, Secretary of Defense, Attorney General, Secretary of the Interior, Secretary of Agriculture, Secretary of Commerce, Secretary of Labor, Secretary of Health, and Human Services, Secretary of Housing and Urban Development, Secretary of Transportation, Secretary of Energy, Secretary of Education, Secretary of Veterans Affairs, and Secretary of Homeland Security.

The Vice President, the Speaker of the House and the President pro tempore of the Senate also attend all cabinet meetings. These eighteen people advise the President on what choices he or she should make.

How important are your rights as an American citizen?

Here are our "BILL OF RIGHTS!"

1. Freedom of Speech, Press and Religion!
2. The Right to bear arms.
3. Citizens do not have to house soldiers.
4. No unreasonable searches and seizures.
5. No double jeopardy. Cannot be made to bear witness against themselves.
6. Right to quick, fair trial, neutral jury, attorney, witnesses in their favor
7. Right to take a matter to court and trial by jury when value exceeds twenty dollars.
8. Bans extreme punishment. No cruel, unusual, excessive fines or bail.
9. You have more rights than listed. Absence doesn't diminish importance.
10. Fed has powers assigned by the Constitution; States control all else.

We may not get all we want in our next president however, we should vote for the one who will do the most for us. I don't believe we should pick a Republican or a Democrat, we should pick a leader who can handle the many problems America has and get us back to peace and prosperity.

We need a president who is strong enough to clean house with our one-sided FBI. It is worse today than when we had J. Edgar Hoover. Alan Dershowitz, famous Harvard Law professor recently stated, "I don't trust the DOJ or the FBI!"

And quite frankly, neither do I! What do you think?

Those in power are not saying they are above the law. They are saying, "We are the law!" and that is very dangerous for all American citizens regardless of your political beliefs.

In September 2022, 69 percent of Americans of both political parties believe our democracy is in danger of collapse! And 70 percent of Americans believe America is going in the wrong direction!

Your choice in 2024 will be a **DICTATORSHIP.**

where the meaning of democracy

allows only one side to speak.

Or **AMERICAN FREEDOM!**

You only have one vote!

Don't waste it! Spend it wisely!

Vote for the person you believe can best

lead us in the right direction.

To repeat President Ronald Reagan's question to the voters during his debate with President Jimmy Carter,

"Are you better off today than you were four years ago?"

We have lived through the presidency of Donald Trump, and we are now living with Joe Biden.

In your search for the best candidate for the Presidency of the United States in 2024, someone who can solve the mess that America is in, it is my belief your best choice who will make is.

. . . .

.

.

.

↓

Donald J. Trump!

And He will put. . .

America First

CHAPTER TWENTY-TWO

Conclusion

As we have traveled through the pages of this book, chances are at times you thought I am a democrat. At other times you may have thought I am a republican.

Believe me, "I am neither!" As stated in the beginning, I choose who's the most qualified candidate who can do what needs to be done for America today.

I believe, the America we love, is under siege.

The Democrats are at war with **TRUMP!**

The Democrats are at war with the **REPUBLICAN PARTY!**

The Democrats are at war with the **REPUBLIC!**

The Democrats are at war with **AMERICA'S FREEDOM!**

Yes, I believe our freedom is being challenged, and we are at risk of losing all the rights promised by our constitution.

America needs "DIRTY HARRY!"

At 6:11 p.m. on JULY 13, 2024, there was an assassination attempt on former president and leading 2024 presidential candidate Donald J. Trump. In the past 100 years there have been at least 17 attempts to assassinate the president or candidate for president of the United States. Two attempts were successful.

There are many questions which will be investigated and hopefully answered for the American public. Who was 20-year-old, Thomas Mathew Crooks? What was his motive? Was he a lone wolf? How did he get in position on a roof 412 feet away with a direct line of sight vantage point to take a shot at Trump?

Crooks

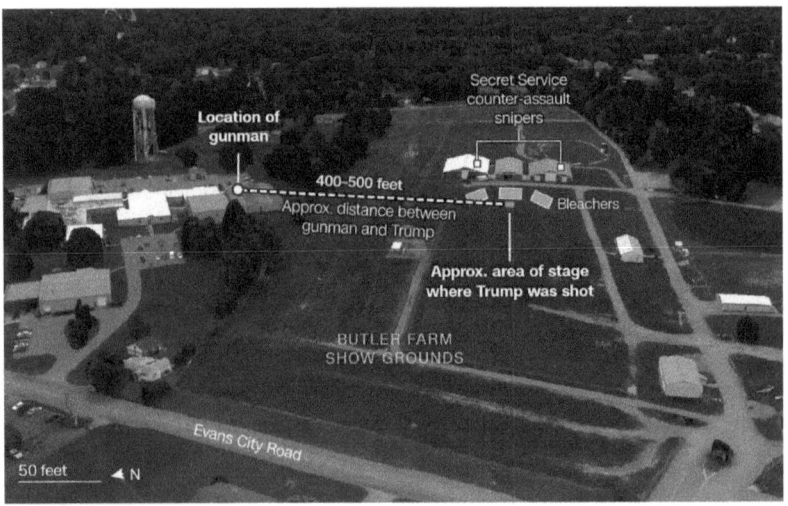

One day following her disastrous appearance at the congressional hearing on July 22, 2024, U.S. Secret Service Director Kimberly Cheadle stepped down after widespread calls from lawmakers for her to resign following the assassination attempt on former President Donald Trump. She will be known as the woman F***ed the Secret Service Security that caused Donald Trump to take a bullet for democracy.

Cheadle

Cory

She also accepted responsibility for the death of Cory Comperatore and the severely wounded others.

An interesting fact: This is the first Trump rally where the Secret Service had snippers present and they shot the shooter dead. If this was a planned assassination, the planners would want the shooter dead and not available to be questioned. This as many other facts lead to the conspiracy beliefs of many Americans. Similar to the JFK assassination the truth may not be known for fifty years, or maybe not at all.

The quarter inch that saved American Freedo0m!

Just imagine, in the length of time for the shooter to pull the trigger on his AR566, Trump turned his head a quarter of an inch. The shot winged the top of Trumps right ear, less than a quarter of an inch from his certain death. This quarter-inch saved Donald J. Trumps life and very possibility saved freedom in America.

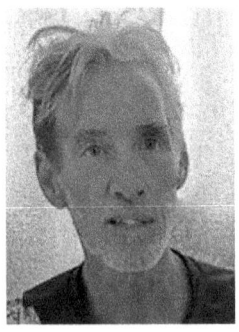

Ryan Westley Routh

Just 64 days after the Butler assassination attempt, a gunman, Ryan Westley Routh, 58, attempted to assassinate Donald Trump on Sunday September 15, 2024, at Trump's golf course in Palm Beach, Florida. The Secret Service said its agents were accompanying Trump on the golf course, when one who was securing holes ahead of Trump spotted a gun barrel in some bushes near the property line. Routh was about 400 to 500 yards away from Trump and hiding in shrubbery. He had been in the area near the golf course for roughly 12 hours.

Agents fired four rounds at Routh. Routh then dropped his AK-47 rifle, two backpacks, a GoPro camera and other items and fled in a black Nissan car. A witness took a photo of Routh's car and license plate and gave it to authorities. Shortly after, sheriff's deputies in neighboring Martin County stopped the suspect on Interstate 95 and took him into custody.

In 2002, at 36-years-old, Ryan Routh had been arrested after a three-hour standoff with law enforcement in which he barricaded himself inside a roofing business. He was charged with possessing a weapon of mass destruction, which was a machine gun. Trump was not shot or injured in this attempt.

They tried to kill Donald Trump two times in two months.

Donald Trump is an American warrior!
He is not dressed in armor. He shows up in suit and tie, fighting for a lifestyle only known to Americans!
A lifestyle built on a foundation of
FREEDOM!

Senator JD Vance from Ohio selected by Trump as Vice Presidential candidate. Vance is a 'Rags to Riches' candidate who has lived the American Dream.

All Americans, Republicans, Democrats, and Independence need to . . .

COME TOGETHER FOR
FREEDOM!

Thank You!

www.ingramcontent.com/pod-product-compliance
Lightning Source LLC
Chambersburg PA
CBHW052027030426
42337CB00027B/4895